MznLnx

Missing Links Exam Preps

Exam Prep for

A First Course In Abstract Algebra

Fraleigh, 7th Edition

The MznLnx Exam Prep is your link from the texbook and lecture to your exams.
The MznLnx Exam Preps are unauthorized and comprehensive reviews of your textbooks.

All material provided by MznLnx and Rico Publications (c) 2010
Textbook publishers and textbook authors do not particpate in or contribute to these reviews.

MznLnx

Rico Publications

Exam Prep for A First Course In Abstract Algebra
7th Edition
Fraleigh

Publisher: Raymond Houge
Assistant Editor: Michael Rouger
Text and Cover Designer: Lisa Buckner
Marketing Manager: Sara Swagger
Project Manager, Editorial Production: Jerry Emerson
Art Director: Vernon Lowerui

Product Manager: Dave Mason
Editorial Assitant: Rachel Guzmanji
Pedagogy: Debra Long
Cover Image: Jim Reed/Getty Images
Text and Cover Printer: City Printing, Inc.
Compositor: Media Mix, Inc.

(c) 2010 Rico Publications

ALL RIGHTS RESERVED. No part of this work covered by the copyright may be reproduced or used in any form or by an means--graphic, electronic, or mechanical, including photocopying, recording, taping, Web distribution, information storage, and retrieval systems, or in any other manner--without the written permission of the publisher.

Printed in the United States
ISBN:

For more information about our products, contact us at:
Dave.Mason@RicoPublications.com

For permission to use material from this text or product, submit a request online to:
Dave.Mason@RicoPublications.com

Contents

CHAPTER 1
GROUPS AND SUBGROUPS — 1

CHAPTER 2
PERMUTATIONS, COSETS, AND DIRECT PRODUCTS — 19

CHAPTER 3
HOMOMORPHISMS AND FACTOR GROUPS — 34

CHAPTER 4
RINGS AND FIELDS — 49

CHAPTER 5
IDEALS AND FACTOR RINGS — 67

CHAPTER 6
EXTENSION FIELDS — 76

CHAPTER 7
ADVANCED GROUP THEORY — 90

CHAPTER 8
GROUPS IN TOPOLOGY — 101

CHAPTER 9
FACTORIZATION — 112

CHAPTER 10
AUTOMORPHISMS AND GALOIS THEORY — 122

ANSWER KEY — 123

TO THE STUDENT

COMPREHENSIVE

The *MznLnx* Exam Prep series is designed to help you pass your exams. Editors at MznLnx review your textbooks and then prepare these practice exams to help you master the textbook material. Unlike study guides, workbooks, and practice tests provided by the texbook publisher and textbook authors, *MznLnx* gives you **all** of the material in each chapter in exam form, not just samples, so you can be sure to nail your exam.

MECHANICAL

The MznLnx Exam Prep series creates exams that will help you learn the subject matter as well as test you on your understanding. Each question is designed to help you master the concept. Just working through the exams, you gain an understanding of the subject--its a simple mechanical process that produces success.

INTEGRATED STUDY GUIDE AND REVIEW

MznLnx is not just a set of exams designed to test you, its also a comprehensive review of the subject content. Each exam question is also a review of the concept, making sure that you will get the answer correct without having to go to other sources of material. You learn as you go! Its the easiest way to pass an exam.

HUMOR

Studying can be tedious and dry. MznLnx's instructional design includes moderate humor within the exam questions on occassion, to break the tedium and revitalize the brain

Chapter 1. GROUPS AND SUBGROUPS

1. In mathematics, _____ is an elementary arithmetic operation. When one of the numbers is a whole number, _____ is the repeated sum of the other number.
   a. Multiplication0
   b. Thing
   c. Undefined
   d. Undefined

2. In mathematics, the _____ inverse of a number x, denoted 1/x or x^{-1}, is the number which, when multiplied by x, yields 1. The _____ inverse of x is also called the reciprocal of x.
   a. Multiplicative0
   b. Thing
   c. Undefined
   d. Undefined

3. In mathematics, a _____ may be described informally as a number that can be given by an infinite decimal representation.
   a. Real number0
   b. Thing
   c. Undefined
   d. Undefined

4. The _____, the average in everyday English, which is also called the arithmetic _____ (and is distinguished from the geometric _____ or harmonic _____). The average is also called the sample _____. The expected value of a random variable, which is also called the population _____.
   a. Thing
   b. Mean0
   c. Undefined
   d. Undefined

5. A _____ is 360° or 2δ radians.
   a. Thing
   b. Turn0
   c. Undefined
   d. Undefined

6. A _____ is a calculation involving two input quantities. It can be accomplished using either a binary function or binary operator.
   a. Binary operation0
   b. Thing
   c. Undefined
   d. Undefined

7. In group theory, given a group G under a binary operation *, we say that some subset H of G is a _____ of G if H also forms a group under the operation *.
   a. Thing
   b. Subgroup0
   c. Undefined
   d. Undefined

8. In mathematics, a _____ is a number in the form of a + bi where a and b are real numbers, and i is the imaginary unit, with the property i 2 = −1. The real number a is called the real part of the _____, and the real number b is the imaginary part.
   a. Thing
   b. Complex number0
   c. Undefined
   d. Undefined

9. A _____ is a set of numbers that designate location in a given reference system, such as x,y in a planar _____ system or an x,y,z in a three-dimensional _____ system.
   a. Thing
   b. Coordinate0
   c. Undefined
   d. Undefined

10. An _____ is a straight line around which a geometric figure can be rotated.

Chapter 1. GROUPS AND SUBGROUPS

   a. Axis0
   c. Undefined
   b. Thing
   d. Undefined

11. In mathematics, the _____ of a coordinate system is the point where the axes of the system intersect.
   a. Thing
   c. Undefined
   b. Origin0
   d. Undefined

12. _____ means of or relating to the French philosopher and mathematician René Descartes.
   a. Cartesian0
   c. Undefined
   b. Thing
   d. Undefined

13. In mathematics, a _____ is a countable collection of open covers of a topological space that satisfies certain separation axioms.
   a. Development0
   c. Undefined
   b. Thing
   d. Undefined

14. In mathematics, a _____ is a polynomial equation of the second degree. The general form is $ax^2 + bx + c = 0$.
   a. Thing
   c. Undefined
   b. Quadratic equation0
   d. Undefined

15. In mathematics, an _____ number is a complex number whose square is a negative real number. They were defined in 1572 by Rafael Bombelli.
   a. Thing
   c. Undefined
   b. Imaginary0
   d. Undefined

16. _____ is the study of terms and their use — of words and compound words that are used in specific contexts.
   a. Thing
   c. Undefined
   b. Terminology0
   d. Undefined

17. In mathematics, a _____ is the result of multiplying, or an expression that identifies factors to be multiplied.
   a. Product0
   c. Undefined
   b. Thing
   d. Undefined

18. _____ or arithmetics is the oldest and most elementary branch of mathematics, used by almost everyone, for tasks ranging from simple daily counting to advanced science and business calculations.
   a. Thing
   c. Undefined
   b. Arithmetic0
   d. Undefined

19. A _____ is a negotiable instrument instructing a financial institution to pay a specific amount of a specific currency from a specific demand account held in the maker/depositor's name with that institution. Both the maker and payee may be natural persons or legal entities.
   a. Check0
   c. Undefined
   b. Thing
   d. Undefined

20. The _____ integers are all the integers from zero on upwards.

a. Nonnegative0
b. Thing
c. Undefined
d. Undefined

21. In mathematics, the _____ (or modulus) of a real number is its numerical value without regard to its sign.
   a. Thing
   b. Absolute value0
   c. Undefined
   d. Undefined

22. A _____ is the sum of the elements of a sequence.
   a. Series0
   b. Thing
   c. Undefined
   d. Undefined

23. Leonhard _____ was a pioneering Swiss mathematician and physicist, who spent most of his life in Russia and Germany.
   a. Euler0
   b. Person
   c. Undefined
   d. Undefined

24. An _____ of a product of sums expresses it as a sum of products by using the fact that multiplication distributes over addition.
   a. Expansion0
   b. Thing
   c. Undefined
   d. Undefined

25. _____ has many meanings, most of which simply .
   a. Thing
   b. Power0
   c. Undefined
   d. Undefined

26. _____ in one variable is an infinite series of the form
   a. Power series0
   b. Thing
   c. Undefined
   d. Undefined

27. In mathematics, the _____ functions are functions of an angle; they are important when studying triangles and modeling periodic phenomena, among many other applications.
   a. Thing
   b. Trigonometric0
   c. Undefined
   d. Undefined

28. _____ is a mathematical operation, written a^n, involving two numbers, the base a and the exponent n.
   a. Exponentiation0
   b. Thing
   c. Undefined
   d. Undefined

29. An _____ is an equality that remains true regardless of the values of any variables that appear within it, to distinguish it from an equality which is true under more particular conditions.
   a. Thing
   b. Identity0
   c. Undefined
   d. Undefined

30. In functional analysis and related areas of mathematics the _____ set of a given subset of a vector space is a certain set in the dual space.

Chapter 1. GROUPS AND SUBGROUPS

    a. Polar0
    c. Undefined
    b. Thing
    d. Undefined

31. The _____ are the only integral domain whose positive elements are well-ordered, and in which order is preserved by addition. Like the natural numbers, the _____ form a countably infinite set. The set of all _____ is usually denoted in mathematics by a boldface Z .
    a. Integers0
    c. Undefined
    b. Thing
    d. Undefined

32. In elementary algebra, an _____ is a set that contains every real number between two indicated numbers and may contain the two numbers themselves.
    a. Interval0
    c. Undefined
    b. Thing
    d. Undefined

33. A _____ is the result of the addition of a set of numbers. The numbers may be natural numbers, complex numbers, matrices, or still more complicated objects. An infinite _____ is a subtle procedure known as a series.
    a. Sum0
    c. Undefined
    b. Thing
    d. Undefined

34. In Euclidean geometry, a _____ is the set of all points in a plane at a fixed distance, called the radius, from a given point, the center.
    a. Thing
    c. Undefined
    b. Circle0
    d. Undefined

35. In mathematics, an _____ (Greek:isos "equal", and morphe "shape") is a bijective map f such that both f and its inverse f $^{-1}$ are homomorphisms, i.e. *structure-preserving* mappings.
    a. Isomorphism0
    c. Undefined
    b. Thing
    d. Undefined

36. An _____ or member of a set is an object that when collected together make up the set.
    a. Element0
    c. Undefined
    b. Thing
    d. Undefined

37. In mathematics, the _____ , or members of a set or more generally a class are all those objects which when collected together make up the set or class.
    a. Elements0
    c. Undefined
    b. Thing
    d. Undefined

38. _____ is a branch of mathematics concerning the study of structure, relation and quantity.
    a. Concept
    c. Undefined
    b. Algebra0
    d. Undefined

39. In Euclidean geometry, an _____ is a closed segment of a differentiable curve in the two-dimensional plane; for example, a circular _____ is a segment of a circle.

a. Concept
b. Arc0
c. Undefined
d. Undefined

40. The _____ is a unit of plane angle. It is represented by the symbol "rad" or, more rarely, by the superscript c (for "circular measure"). For example, an angle of 1.2 radians would be written "1.2 rad" or "1.2c" (second symbol can produce confusion with centigrads).
    a. Radian0
    b. Thing
    c. Undefined
    d. Undefined

41. _____ is a unit of plane angle, equal to 180/δ degrees, or about 57.2958 degrees
    a. Thing
    b. Radian measure0
    c. Undefined
    d. Undefined

42. In classical geometry, a _____ of a circle or sphere is any line segment from its center to its boundary. By extension, the _____ of a circle or sphere is the length of any such segment. The _____ is half the diameter. In science and engineering the term _____ of curvature is commonly used as a synonym for _____.
    a. Radius0
    b. Thing
    c. Undefined
    d. Undefined

43. The _____ is the distance around a closed curve. _____ is a kind of perimeter.
    a. Circumference0
    b. Thing
    c. Undefined
    d. Undefined

44. A _____ is a function that assigns a number to subsets of a given set.
    a. Thing
    b. Measure0
    c. Undefined
    d. Undefined

45. _____ is an adjective usually refering to being in the centre.
    a. Central0
    b. Thing
    c. Undefined
    d. Undefined

46. In mathematics, science including computer science, linguistics and engineering, an _____ is, generally speaking, an independent variable or input to a function.
    a. Argument0
    b. Thing
    c. Undefined
    d. Undefined

47. An _____ of a number a is a number b such that $b^n=a$.
    a. Nth root0
    b. Thing
    c. Undefined
    d. Undefined

48. In mathematics, a _____ of a complex-valued function f is a member x of the domain of f such that f(x) vanishes at x, that is, $x : f(x) = 0$.
    a. Root0
    b. Thing
    c. Undefined
    d. Undefined

Chapter 1. GROUPS AND SUBGROUPS

49. In mathematics, the nth _____ are all the complex numbers which yield 1 when raised to a given power n. It can be shown that they are located on the unit circle of the complex plane and that in that plane they form the vertices of an n-sided regular polygon with one vertex on 1.
    a. Thing
    b. Roots of unity0
    c. Undefined
    d. Undefined

50. An _____ is a combination of numbers, operators, grouping symbols and/or free variables and bound variables arranged in a meaningful way which can be evaluated..
    a. Thing
    b. Expression0
    c. Undefined
    d. Undefined

51. In abstract algebra, something that is _____ over a ring is a generalization of the notion of vector space, where instead of requiring the scalars to lie in a field, the "scalars" may lie in an arbitrary ring.
    a. Concept
    b. Modular0
    c. Undefined
    d. Undefined

52. In mathematics, the conjugate _____ or adjoint matrix of an m-by-n matrix A with complex entries is the n-by-m matrix A* obtained from A by taking the transpose and then taking the complex conjugate of each entry.
    a. Thing
    b. Pairs0
    c. Undefined
    d. Undefined

53. An _____ is a collection of two not necessarily distinct objects, one of which is distinguished as the first coordinate and the other as the second coordinate.
    a. Ordered pair0
    b. Thing
    c. Undefined
    d. Undefined

54. The mathematical concept of a _____ expresses the intuitive idea of deterministic dependence between two quantities, one of which is viewed as primary and the other as secondary. A _____ then is a way to associate a unique output for each input of a specified type, for example, a real number or an element of a given set.
    a. Function0
    b. Thing
    c. Undefined
    d. Undefined

55. A _____ is a set whose members are members of another set or a set contained within another set.
    a. Subset0
    b. Thing
    c. Undefined
    d. Undefined

56. In a mathematical proof or a syllogism, a _____ is a statement that is the logical consequence of preceding statements.
    a. Conclusion0
    b. Concept
    c. Undefined
    d. Undefined

57. The word _____ comes from the Latin word linearis, which means created by lines.
    a. Thing
    b. Linear0
    c. Undefined
    d. Undefined

Chapter 1. GROUPS AND SUBGROUPS

58. In mathematics, a _____ is a rectangular table of numbers or, more generally, a table consisting of abstract quantities that can be added and multiplied.
    a. Thing
    b. Matrix0
    c. Undefined
    d. Undefined

59. In mathematics, a _____ of a k-place relation $L \subseteq X_1 \times ... \times X_k$ is one of the sets X_j, $1 \le j \le k$. In the special case where k = 2 and $L \subseteq X_1 \times X_2$ is a function $L : X_1 \to X_2$, it is conventional to refer to X_1 as the _____ of the function and to refer to X_2 as the codomain of the function.
    a. Domain0
    b. Thing
    c. Undefined
    d. Undefined

60. In common philosophical language, a proposition or _____, is the content of an assertion, that is, it is true-or-false and defined by the meaning of a particular piece of language.
    a. Concept
    b. Statement0
    c. Undefined
    d. Undefined

61. In mathematics, a _____ is a statement that can be proved on the basis of explicitly stated or previously agreed assumptions.
    a. Theorem0
    b. Thing
    c. Undefined
    d. Undefined

62. _____, either of the curved-bracket punctuation marks that together make a set of _____
    a. Parentheses0
    b. Thing
    c. Undefined
    d. Undefined

63. In mathematics, a _____ of a positive integer n is a way of writing n as a sum of positive integers.
    a. Thing
    b. Composition0
    c. Undefined
    d. Undefined

64. In mathematics, _____ is a property that a binary operation can have. Within an expression containing two or more of the same associative operators in a row, the order of operations does not matter as long as the sequence of the operands is not changed.
    a. Thing
    b. Associativity0
    c. Undefined
    d. Undefined

65. In mathematics, a _____ is a demonstration that, assuming certain axioms, some statement is necessarily true.
    a. Thing
    b. Proof0
    c. Undefined
    d. Undefined

66. Mathematical _____ is used to represent ideas.
    a. Notation0
    b. Thing
    c. Undefined
    d. Undefined

67. _____ is the addition of a set of numbers; the result is their sum. The "numbers" to be summed may be natural numbers, complex numbers, matrices, or still more complicated objects. An infinite sum is a subtle procedure known as a series.

Chapter 1. GROUPS AND SUBGROUPS

a. Summation0
b. Thing
c. Undefined
d. Undefined

68. In mathematics, a _____ number is a number which can be expressed as a ratio of two integers. Non-integer _____ numbers (commonly called fractions) are usually written as the vulgar fraction a / b, where b is not zero.
    a. Thing
    b. Rational0
    c. Undefined
    d. Undefined

69. In mathematics, an inequality is a statement about the relative size or order of two objects. For example 14 > 10, or 14 is _____ 10.
    a. Greater than0
    b. Thing
    c. Undefined
    d. Undefined

70. In mathematics, a _____ is an n-tuple with n being 3.
    a. Thing
    b. Triple0
    c. Undefined
    d. Undefined

71. In logic, and especially in its applications to mathematics and philosophy, a _____ is an exception to a proposed general rule, i.e., a specific instance of the falsity of a universal quantification (a "for all" statement).
    a. Thing
    b. Counterexample0
    c. Undefined
    d. Undefined

72. _____ is a property that a binary operation can have.
    a. Associative law0
    b. Thing
    c. Undefined
    d. Undefined

73. In abstract algebra, a _____ is a structure-preserving map between two algebraic structures. The word _____ comes from the Greek language: homo meaning "same" and morphi meaning "shape".
    a. Thing
    b. Homomorphism0
    c. Undefined
    d. Undefined

74. An _____ is a binary relation between two elements of a set which groups them together as being equivalent in some way.
    a. Equivalence relation0
    b. Thing
    c. Undefined
    d. Undefined

75. _____ is a mathematical operation, written a^n, involving two numbers, the base a and the exponent n.
    a. Thing
    b. Exponentiating0
    c. Undefined
    d. Undefined

76. _____ is the logarithm to the base e, where e is an irrational constant approximately equal to 2.718281828459.
    a. Natural logarithm0
    b. Thing
    c. Undefined
    d. Undefined

77. In mathematics, a _____ of a number x is the exponent y of the power by such that $x = b^y$. The value used for the base b must be neither 0 nor 1, nor a root of 1 in the case of the extension to complex numbers, and is typically 10, e, or 2.

Chapter 1. GROUPS AND SUBGROUPS

a. Logarithm0
b. Thing
c. Undefined
d. Undefined

78. The _____ of a ring R is defined to be the smallest positive integer n such that $n\,a = 0$, for all a in R.
a. Characteristic0
b. Thing
c. Undefined
d. Undefined

79. In mathematics, an _____ (or neutral element) is a special type of element of a set with respect to a binary operation on that set.
a. Identity element0
b. Concept
c. Undefined
d. Undefined

80. The _____ is a measurement of how a function changes when the values of its inputs change.
a. Thing
b. Derivative0
c. Undefined
d. Undefined

81. In algebra, a _____ is a function depending on n that associates a scalar, det(A), to every $n \times n$ square matrix A.
a. Determinant0
b. Thing
c. Undefined
d. Undefined

82. Acid _____ ratio measures the ability of a company to use its near cash or quick assets to immediately extinguish its current liabilities.
a. Test0
b. Thing
c. Undefined
d. Undefined

83. In mathematics, a set is called _____ if there is a bijection between the set and some set of the form {1, 2, ..., n} where n is a natural number.
a. Thing
b. Finite0
c. Undefined
d. Undefined

84. In mathematics, a _____ occurs if there is a bijection between the set and some set of the form 1, 2, ..., n where n is a natural number.
a. Concept
b. Finite set0
c. Undefined
d. Undefined

85. A _____ is a number that is less than zero.
a. Thing
b. Negative number0
c. Undefined
d. Undefined

86. A _____ is an equation in which each term is either a constant or the product of a constant times the first power of a variable.
a. Linear equation0
b. Thing
c. Undefined
d. Undefined

87. In mathematics, the _____ inverse, or opposite, of a number n is the number that, when added to n, yields zero. The _____ inverse of n is denoted −n.

a. Additive0
b. Thing
c. Undefined
d. Undefined

88. _____ element of an element x with respect to a binary operation * with identity element e is an element y such that x * y = y * x = e. In particular,
   a. Thing
   b. Inverse0
   c. Undefined
   d. Undefined

89. Deductive _____ is the kind of _____ in which the conclusion is necessitated by, or reached from, previously known facts (the premises).
   a. Reasoning0
   b. Thing
   c. Undefined
   d. Undefined

90. In mathematics, a _____ in elementary terms is any of a variety of different functions from geometry, such as rotations, reflections and translations.
   a. Transformation0
   b. Thing
   c. Undefined
   d. Undefined

91. In mathematics, an _____ is something that does not change under a set of transformations. The property of being an _____ is invariance.
   a. Invariant0
   b. Thing
   c. Undefined
   d. Undefined

92. _____ is the branch of pure mathematics concerned with the properties of numbers in general, and integers in particular, as well as the wider classes of problems that arise from their study.
   a. Number theory0
   b. Thing
   c. Undefined
   d. Undefined

93. In mathematics, a _____ number (or a _____) is a natural number that has exactly two (distinct) natural number divisors, which are 1 and the _____ number itself.
   a. Thing
   b. Prime0
   c. Undefined
   d. Undefined

94. _____ was a pioneering Swiss mathematician and physicist, who spent most of his life in Russia and Germany.
   a. Leonhard Euler0
   b. Person
   c. Undefined
   d. Undefined

95. A _____ is the part of the dividend that is left over when the dividend is not evenly divisible by the divisor.
   a. Remainder0
   b. Thing
   c. Undefined
   d. Undefined

96. _____ is the rearrangement of objects or symbols into distinguishable sequences.
   a. Permutation0
   b. Thing
   c. Undefined
   d. Undefined

97. _____, a Norwegian mathematician, was born in Nedstrand, near Finnoy where his father acted as rector.

Chapter 1. GROUPS AND SUBGROUPS

    a. Niels Henrik Abel0   b. Person
    c. Undefined   d. Undefined

98. In mathematics, an abelian group, also called a _____, is a group G, * such that a * b = b * a for all a and b in G. In other words, the order in which the binary operation is performed doesn't matter.
    a. Commutative group0   b. Thing
    c. Undefined   d. Undefined

99. In mathematics, a _____ is an expression that is constructed from one or more variables and constants, using only the operations of addition, subtraction, multiplication, and constant positive whole number exponents. is a _____. Note in particular that division by an expression containing a variable is not in general allowed in polynomials. [1]
    a. Thing   b. Polynomial0
    c. Undefined   d. Undefined

100. _____ is the symbold used to indicate the nth root of a number
    a. Radical0   b. Thing
    c. Undefined   d. Undefined

101. In mathematics, _____ are used to indicate the square root of a number.
    a. Thing   b. Radicals0
    c. Undefined   d. Undefined

102. In mathematics, a _____ is any function which can be written as the ratio of two polynomial functions.
    a. Rational function0   b. Thing
    c. Undefined   d. Undefined

103. The _____ is a rule which states that when you add or multiply numbers, changing the order doesn't change the result.
    a. Thing   b. Commutative law0
    c. Undefined   d. Undefined

104. Marie Ennemond _____ was a French mathematician, known both for his foundational work in group theory and for his influential Cours d'analyse. He was born in Lyon and educated at the École polytechnique. He was an engineer by profession; later in life he taught at the École polytechnique and the Collège de France; where he had a reputation for eccentric choices of notation.
    a. Camille Jordan0   b. Thing
    c. Undefined   d. Undefined

105. In mathematics, an _____ .
    a. Ellipse0   b. Thing
    c. Undefined   d. Undefined

106. In mathematics, an _____, also called a commutative group, is a group such that a * b= b*a for all and b in G. In other words, the order in which the binary operation is performed doesnt matter.

a. Abelian group0
b. Thing
c. Undefined
d. Undefined

107. The _____ of equality is the formal name for the property of equality that allows one to add the same quantity to both sides of an equation.
   a. Concept
   b. Additive property0
   c. Undefined
   d. Undefined

108. In physics and in _____ calculus, a spatial _____, or simply _____, is a concept characterized by a magnitude and a direction.
   a. Thing
   b. Vector0
   c. Undefined
   d. Undefined

109. _____ is a collection of objects called vectors that, informally speaking, may be scaled and added.
   a. Vector space0
   b. Thing
   c. Undefined
   d. Undefined

110. _____ is a set, with some particular properties and usually some additional structure, such as the operations of addition or multiplication, for instance.
   a. Space0
   b. Thing
   c. Undefined
   d. Undefined

111. An _____ is any starting assumption from which other statements are logically derived
   a. Axiom0
   b. Thing
   c. Undefined
   d. Undefined

112. In mathematics, the idea of _____ generalises the concepts of negation, in relation to addition, and reciprocal, in relation to multiplication.
   a. Thing
   b. Inverse element0
   c. Undefined
   d. Undefined

113. In mathematics, a linear map also called a _____ or linear operator is a function between two vector spaces that preserves the operations of vector addition and scalar multiplication.
   a. Linear transformation0
   b. Thing
   c. Undefined
   d. Undefined

114. In mathematics, there are several meanings of _____ depending on the subject.
   a. Thing
   b. Degree0
   c. Undefined
   d. Undefined

115. In mathematics, a matrix can be thought of as each row or _____ being a vector. Hence, a space formed by row vectors or _____ vectors are said to be a row space or a _____ space.
   a. Concept
   b. Column0
   c. Undefined
   d. Undefined

Chapter 1. GROUPS AND SUBGROUPS

116. In plane geometry, a _____ is a polygon with four equal sides, four right angles, and parallel opposite sides. In algebra, the _____ of a number is that number multiplied by itself.
 a. Thing
 b. Square0
 c. Undefined
 d. Undefined

117. In linear algebra, the _____ of a square matrix is the diagonal which runs from the top left corner to the bottom right corner.
 a. Thing
 b. Main diagonal0
 c. Undefined
 d. Undefined

118. A _____ can refer to a line joining two nonadjacent vertices of a polygon or polyhedron, or in some contexts any upward or downward sloping line. .
 a. Diagonal0
 b. Thing
 c. Undefined
 d. Undefined

119. _____ is a square matrix in which the entries outside the main diagonal are all zero.
 a. Thing
 b. Diagonal matrix0
 c. Undefined
 d. Undefined

120. In mathematics, the notion of _____ is a generalization of the notion of invertible.
 a. Cancellation0
 b. Thing
 c. Undefined
 d. Undefined

121. In mathematics and computer science, the concept of _____ arises in a number of places in abstract algebra; in particular, in the theory of projectors, closure operators and functional programming, in which it is connected to the property of referential transparency.
 a. Idempotence0
 b. Thing
 c. Undefined
 d. Undefined

122. _____ is that branch of mathematics concerned with the study of groups. These are sets with a rule, or operation. The operation in a group must satisfy closure and have these three additional properties: 1) The operation must have the property of associativity. 2) There must be an identity element. 3) Every element must have a corresponding inverse element. _____ is used throughout mathematics and has several applications in physics and chemistry. Groups can be finite or infinite. A classification of finite simple groups, completed in 1983, is one of the major achievements of mathematics in the 20th century.
 a. Thing
 b. Group theory0
 c. Undefined
 d. Undefined

123. _____ are objects, characters, or other concrete representations of ideas, concepts, or other abstractions.
 a. Symbols0
 b. Thing
 c. Undefined
 d. Undefined

124. In mathematics the _____ of a set which is equipped with the operation of addition is an element which, when added to any other element x in the set, yields x.

Chapter 1. GROUPS AND SUBGROUPS

    a. Concept
    c. Undefined
    b. Additive identity0
    d. Undefined

125. In mathematics, factorization (British English: factorisation) or factoring is the decomposition of an object (for example, a number, a polynomial, or a matrix) into a product of other objects, or _____, which when multiplied together give the original.
    a. Factors0
    c. Undefined
    b. Thing
    d. Undefined

126. _____ are groups whose members are members of another set or a set contained within another set.
    a. Thing
    c. Undefined
    b. Subsets0
    d. Undefined

127. A _____ fraction is a fraction in which the absolute value of the numerator is less than the denominator--hence, the absolute value of the fraction is less than 1.
    a. Thing
    c. Undefined
    b. Proper0
    d. Undefined

128. In linear algebra, a _____ is a 1 × n matrix, that is, a matrix consisting of a single row
    a. Row vector0
    c. Undefined
    b. Thing
    d. Undefined

129. In mathematics, in the field of group theory, a _____ of a group is a quasisimple subnormal subgroup.
    a. Concept
    c. Undefined
    b. Component0
    d. Undefined

130. A _____ function is a function for which, intuitively, small changes in the input result in small changes in the output.
    a. Continuous0
    c. Undefined
    b. Event
    d. Undefined

131. _____ the expected value of a random variable displays the average or central value of the variable.It is a summary value of the distribution of the variable.
    a. Thing
    c. Undefined
    b. Determining0
    d. Undefined

132. In mathematics, a subset of Euclidean space R^n is called _____ if it is closed and bounded.
    a. Compact0
    c. Undefined
    b. Thing
    d. Undefined

133. In group theory, a _____ or monogenous group is a group that can be generated by a single element, in the sense that the group has an element g called a "generator" of the group such that, when written multiplicatively, every element of the group is a power of g a multiple of g when the notation is additive.
    a. Thing
    c. Undefined
    b. Cyclic group0
    d. Undefined

Chapter 1. GROUPS AND SUBGROUPS

134. In mathematics, _____ is synonymous with perpendicular when used as a simple adjective that is not part of any longer phrase with a standard definition. It means at right angles. It comes from the Greek ἀξί ὀρθί, orthos, meaning "straight", used by Euclid to mean right; and γωνία gonia, meaning angle. Two streets that cross each other at a right angle are _____ to one another.
   a. Orthogonal0
   b. Thing
   c. Undefined
   d. Undefined

135. In linear algebra, the _____ of a matrix A is another matrix AT
   a. Transpose0
   b. Thing
   c. Undefined
   d. Undefined

136. In mathematics and the mathematical sciences, a _____ is a fixed, but possibly unspecified, value. This is in contrast to a variable, which is not fixed.
   a. Thing
   b. Constant0
   c. Undefined
   d. Undefined

137. _____ is a function whose values do not vary and thus are constant.
   a. Thing
   b. Constant function0
   c. Undefined
   d. Undefined

138. In geometry, the _____ of an object is a point in some sense in the middle of the object.
   a. Center0
   b. Thing
   c. Undefined
   d. Undefined

139. A frame of _____ is a particular perspective from which the universe is observed.
   a. Thing
   b. Reference0
   c. Undefined
   d. Undefined

140. In mathematics, the _____ of two sets A and B is the set that contains all elements of A that also belong to B (or equivalently, all elements of B that also belong to A), but no other elements.
   a. Thing
   b. Intersection0
   c. Undefined
   d. Undefined

141. _____ is the state of being greater than any finite real or natural number, however large.
   a. Thing
   b. Infinite0
   c. Undefined
   d. Undefined

142. In mathematics, computing, linguistics, and related disciplines, an _____ is a finite list of well-defined instructions for accomplishing some task which, given an initial state, will terminate in a defined end-state.
   a. Algorithm0
   b. Concept
   c. Undefined
   d. Undefined

143. The _____ is a theorem in mathematics which precisely expresses the outcome of the usual process of division of integers. The name is something of a misnomer, as it is a theorem, not an algorithm, i.e. a well-defined procedure for achieving a specific task — although the _____ can be used to find the greatest common divisor of two integers.

a. Thing
c. Undefined
b. Division Algorithm0
d. Undefined

144. The deductive-nomological model is a formalized view of scientific _____ in natural language.
   a. Explanation0
   b. Thing
   c. Undefined
   d. Undefined

145. A _____ of a number is the product of that number with any integer.
   a. Thing
   b. Multiple0
   c. Undefined
   d. Undefined

146. _____ is the study of geometry using the principles of algebra. _____ can be explained more simply: it is concerned with defining geometrical shapes in a numerical way and extracting numerical information from that representation.
   a. Thing
   b. Analytic geometry0
   c. Undefined
   d. Undefined

147. In mathematics, a _____ is the end result of a division problem. It can also be expressed as the number of times the divisor divides into the dividend.
   a. Quotient0
   b. Thing
   c. Undefined
   d. Undefined

148. A _____ is a mathematical statement which follows easily from a previously proven statement, typically a mathematical theorem.
   a. Thing
   b. Corollary0
   c. Undefined
   d. Undefined

149. In mathematics, the _____ divisor of two non-zero integers, is the largest positive integer that divides both numbers without remainder.
   a. Thing
   b. Greatest common0
   c. Undefined
   d. Undefined

150. In mathematics, a _____ of an integer n, also called a factor of n, is an integer which evenly divides n without leaving a remainder.
   a. Divisor0
   b. Thing
   c. Undefined
   d. Undefined

151. The _____ of measurement are a globally standardized and modernized form of the metric system.
   a. Units0
   b. Thing
   c. Undefined
   d. Undefined

152. A _____ is a simplified and structured visual representation of concepts, ideas, constructions, relations, statistical data, anatomy etc used in all aspects of human activities to visualize and clarify the topic.
   a. Diagram0
   b. Thing
   c. Undefined
   d. Undefined

Chapter 1. GROUPS AND SUBGROUPS

153. In mathematics, an _____ is an isomorphism from a mathematical objct of itself while preserving all of its structure.
   a. Thing
   b. Automorphism0
   c. Undefined
   d. Undefined

154. The _____ of two integers is the smallest positive integer that is a multiple of both intergers.
   a. Thing
   b. Least common multiple0
   c. Undefined
   d. Undefined

155. _____ is a natural number that has exactly two distinct natural number divisors, which are 1 and the _____ itself.
   a. Thing
   b. Prime number0
   c. Undefined
   d. Undefined

156. The _____ of a function is an extension of the concept of a sum, and are identified or found through the use of integration.
   a. Integral0
   b. Thing
   c. Undefined
   d. Undefined

157. In abstract algebra, a _____ G is a subset S such that every element of G can be expressed as the product of finitely many elements of S and their inverses.
   a. Generating set of a group0
   b. Thing
   c. Undefined
   d. Undefined

158. In mathematics, the additive inverse, or _____ of a number n is the number that, when added to n, yields zero. The additive inverse of n is denoted −n. For example, 7 is −7, because 7 + (−7) = 0, and the additive inverse of −0.3 is 0.3, because −0.3 + 0.3 = 0.
   a. Opposite0
   b. Thing
   c. Undefined
   d. Undefined

159. In mathematics, the _____ of a number n is the number that, when added to n, yields zero. The _____ of n is denoted −n. For example, 7 is −7, because 7 + (−7) = 0, and the _____ of −0.3 is 0.3, because −0.3 + 0.3 = 0.
   a. Additive inverse0
   b. Thing
   c. Undefined
   d. Undefined

160. A _____ or digraph G is an ordered pair G: = withV is a set, whose elements are called vertices or nodes, A is a set of ordered pairs of vertices, called directed edges, arcs, or arrows.
   a. Directed graph0
   b. Thing
   c. Undefined
   d. Undefined

161. In geometry, a _____ is a special kind of point, usually a corner of a polygon, polyhedron, or higher dimensional polytope. In the geometry of curves a _____ is a point of where the first derivative of curvature is zero. In graph theory, a _____ is the fundamental unit out of which graphs are formed
   a. Thing
   b. Vertex0
   c. Undefined
   d. Undefined

162. In mathematics, _____ geometry was the traditional name for the geometry of three-dimensional Euclidean space — for practical purposes the kind of space we live in.
 a. Solid0
 b. Thing
 c. Undefined
 d. Undefined

163. _____ means in succession or back-to-back
 a. Thing
 b. Consecutive0
 c. Undefined
 d. Undefined

164. In mathematics, a _____ is an ordered list of objects. Like a set, it contains members, also called elements or terms, and the number of terms is called the length of the _____. Unlike a set, order matters, and the exact same elements can appear multiple times at different positions in the _____.
 a. Sequence0
 b. Thing
 c. Undefined
 d. Undefined

165. _____ is the transport of people on a trip/journey or the process or time involved in a person or object moving from one location to another.
 a. Travel0
 b. Thing
 c. Undefined
 d. Undefined

166. _____ means "constancy", i.e. if something retains a certain feature even after we change a way of looking at it, then it is symmetric.
 a. Symmetry0
 b. Thing
 c. Undefined
 d. Undefined

167. A _____ is one of the basic shapes of geometry: a polygon with three vertices and three sides which are straight line segments.
 a. Triangle0
 b. Thing
 c. Undefined
 d. Undefined

Chapter 2. PERMUTATIONS, COSETS, AND DIRECT PRODUCTS

1. An _____ or member of a set is an object that when collected together make up the set.
   a. Thing
   b. Element0
   c. Undefined
   d. Undefined

2. In mathematics, the _____ , or members of a set or more generally a class are all those objects which when collected together make up the set or class.
   a. Thing
   b. Elements0
   c. Undefined
   d. Undefined

3. A _____ is a calculation involving two input quantities. It can be accomplished using either a binary function or binary operator.
   a. Thing
   b. Binary operation0
   c. Undefined
   d. Undefined

4. In mathematics, a _____ of a positive integer n is a way of writing n as a sum of positive integers.
   a. Composition0
   b. Thing
   c. Undefined
   d. Undefined

5. The mathematical concept of a _____ expresses the intuitive idea of deterministic dependence between two quantities, one of which is viewed as primary and the other as secondary. A _____ then is a way to associate a unique output for each input of a specified type, for example, a real number or an element of a given set.
   a. Function0
   b. Thing
   c. Undefined
   d. Undefined

6. In mathematics, a _____, formed by the composition of one function on another, represents the application of the former to the result of the application of the latter to the argument of the composite.
   a. Function composition0
   b. Thing
   c. Undefined
   d. Undefined

7. A _____ is 360° or 2∂ radians.
   a. Thing
   b. Turn0
   c. Undefined
   d. Undefined

8. In mathematics, a matrix can be thought of as each row or _____ being a vector. Hence, a space formed by row vectors or _____ vectors are said to be a row space or a _____ space.
   a. Concept
   b. Column0
   c. Undefined
   d. Undefined

9. _____ is the rearrangement of objects or symbols into distinguishable sequences.
   a. Permutation0
   b. Thing
   c. Undefined
   d. Undefined

10. In mathematics, a _____ is the result of multiplying, or an expression that identifies factors to be multiplied.
    a. Product0
    b. Thing
    c. Undefined
    d. Undefined

Chapter 2. PERMUTATIONS, COSETS, AND DIRECT PRODUCTS

11. In mathematics, if G is a group, H a subgroup of G, and g an element of G, then, gH = {gh : h an element of H } is a left _____ of H in G, and Hg = {hg : h an element of H } is a right _____ of H in G.
    a. Thing
    b. Coset0
    c. Undefined
    d. Undefined

12. In mathematics and logic, a _____ proof is a way of showing the truth or falsehood of a given statement by a straightforward combination of established facts, usually existing lemmas and theorems, without making any further assumptions.
    a. Direct0
    b. Thing
    c. Undefined
    d. Undefined

13. In mathematics, _____ is an elementary arithmetic operation. When one of the numbers is a whole number, _____ is the repeated sum of the other number.
    a. Multiplication0
    b. Thing
    c. Undefined
    d. Undefined

14. A _____ number is a positive integer which has a positive divisor other than one or itself.
    a. Composite0
    b. Thing
    c. Undefined
    d. Undefined

15. A _____, formed by the composition of one function on another, represents the application of the former to the result of the application of the latter to the argument of the composite.
    a. Thing
    b. Composite function0
    c. Undefined
    d. Undefined

16. _____ has many meanings, most of which simply .
    a. Thing
    b. Power0
    c. Undefined
    d. Undefined

17. In physics, _____ is an influence that may cause an object to accelerate. It may be experienced as a lift, a push, or a pull. The actual acceleration of the body is determined by the vector sum of all forces acting on it, known as net _____ or resultant _____.
    a. Force0
    b. Thing
    c. Undefined
    d. Undefined

18. _____ is the mathematical action of repeatedly adding or subtracting one, usually to find out how many objects there are or to set aside a desired number of objects.
    a. Counting0
    b. Thing
    c. Undefined
    d. Undefined

19. In mathematics, a _____ is a demonstration that, assuming certain axioms, some statement is necessarily true.
    a. Thing
    b. Proof0
    c. Undefined
    d. Undefined

20. Mathematical _____ are demonstrations that, assuming certain axioms, some statement is necessarily true.

Chapter 2. PERMUTATIONS, COSETS, AND DIRECT PRODUCTS

a. Proofs0
b. Thing
c. Undefined
d. Undefined

21. In combinatorial mathematics, a _____ is an un-ordered collection of unique elements.
    a. Combination0
    b. Concept
    c. Undefined
    d. Undefined

22. In mathematics, a _____ of a complex-valued function f is a member x of the domain of f such that f(x) vanishes at x, that is, x : f (x) = 0.
    a. Root0
    b. Thing
    c. Undefined
    d. Undefined

23. In mathematics, a set is called _____ if there is a bijection between the set and some set of the form {1, 2, ..., n} where n is a natural number.
    a. Thing
    b. Finite0
    c. Undefined
    d. Undefined

24. In mathematics, a _____ occurs if there is a bijection between the set and some set of the form 1, 2, ..., n where n is a natural number.
    a. Concept
    b. Finite set0
    c. Undefined
    d. Undefined

25. In mathematics, a _____ is an expression that is constructed from one or more variables and constants, using only the operations of addition, subtraction, multiplication, and constant positive whole number exponents. is a _____. Note in particular that division by an expression containing a variable is not in general allowed in polynomials. [1]
    a. Polynomial0
    b. Thing
    c. Undefined
    d. Undefined

26. In mathematics, a _____ is a statement that can be proved on the basis of explicitly stated or previously agreed assumptions.
    a. Thing
    b. Theorem0
    c. Undefined
    d. Undefined

27. The _____ functions is determined by the nesting of two or more functions to form a single new function.
    a. Thing
    b. Composition of two0
    c. Undefined
    d. Undefined

28. An _____ is an equality that remains true regardless of the values of any variables that appear within it, to distinguish it from an equality which is true under more particular conditions.
    a. Thing
    b. Identity0
    c. Undefined
    d. Undefined

29. _____ element of an element x with respect to a binary operation * with identity element e is an element y such that x * y = y * x = e. In particular,

Chapter 2. PERMUTATIONS, COSETS, AND DIRECT PRODUCTS

a. Thing
c. Undefined
b. Inverse0
d. Undefined

30. An _____ is a function which does the reverse of a given function.
a. Inverse function0
c. Undefined
b. Thing
d. Undefined

31. A _____ is a negotiable instrument instructing a financial institution to pay a specific amount of a specific currency from a specific demand account held in the maker/depositor's name with that institution. Both the maker and payee may be natural persons or legal entities.
a. Check0
c. Undefined
b. Thing
d. Undefined

32. In mathematics, an _____ (Greek:isos "equal", and morphe "shape") is a bijective map f such that both f and its inverse f^{-1} are homomorphisms, i.e. *structure-preserving* mappings.
a. Thing
c. Undefined
b. Isomorphism0
d. Undefined

33. A _____ is one of the basic shapes of geometry: a polygon with three vertices and three sides which are straight line segments.
a. Thing
c. Undefined
b. Triangle0
d. Undefined

34. In geometry, a _____ is a special kind of point, usually a corner of a polygon, polyhedron, or higher dimensional polytope. In the geometry of curves a _____ is a point of where the first derivative of curvature is zero. In graph theory, a _____ is the fundamental unit out of which graphs are formed
a. Thing
c. Undefined
b. Vertex0
d. Undefined

35. In geometry, an _____ polygon is a polygon which has all sides of the same length.
a. Thing
c. Undefined
b. Equilateral0
d. Undefined

36. An _____ is a triangle in which all sides are of equal length.
a. Equilateral triangle0
c. Undefined
b. Thing
d. Undefined

37. In mathematics, _____ is a part of the set theoretic notion of function.
a. Thing
c. Undefined
b. Image0
d. Undefined

38. A _____ is a movement of an object in a circular motion. A two-dimensional object rotates around a center (or point) of _____. A three-dimensional object rotates around a line called an axis. If the axis of _____ is within the body, the body is said to rotate upon itself, or spin—which implies relative speed and perhaps free-movement with angular momentum. A circular motion about an external point, e.g. the Earth about the Sun, is called an orbit or more properly an orbital revolution.

Chapter 2. PERMUTATIONS, COSETS, AND DIRECT PRODUCTS

a. Thing
b. Rotation0
c. Undefined
d. Undefined

39. Mathematical _____ is used to represent ideas.
a. Thing
b. Notation0
c. Undefined
d. Undefined

40. In mathematics, the _____ of order 2n is the abstract group of which one representation is the symmetry group in 2D of a regular polygon with n sides
a. Dihedral group0
b. Thing
c. Undefined
d. Undefined

41. _____ means "constancy", i.e. if something retains a certain feature even after we change a way of looking at it, then it is symmetric.
a. Symmetry0
b. Thing
c. Undefined
d. Undefined

42. In plane geometry, a _____ is a polygon with four equal sides, four right angles, and parallel opposite sides. In algebra, the _____ of a number is that number multiplied by itself.
a. Square0
b. Thing
c. Undefined
d. Undefined

43. In geometry, two lines or planes if one falls on the other in such a way as to create congruent adjacent angles. The term may be used as a noun or adjective. Thus, referring to Figure 1, the line AB is the _____ to CD through the point B.
a. Thing
b. Perpendicular0
c. Undefined
d. Undefined

44. A _____ can refer to a line joining two nonadjacent vertices of a polygon or polyhedron, or in some contexts any upward or downward sloping line. .
a. Thing
b. Diagonal0
c. Undefined
d. Undefined

45. In group theory, given a group G under a binary operation *, we say that some subset H of G is a _____ of G if H also forms a group under the operation *.
a. Subgroup0
b. Thing
c. Undefined
d. Undefined

46. In logic, and especially in its applications to mathematics and philosophy, a _____ is an exception to a proposed general rule, i.e., a specific instance of the falsity of a universal quantification (a "for all" statement).
a. Counterexample0
b. Thing
c. Undefined
d. Undefined

47. In mathematics, a _____ is a mathematical statement which appears likely to be true, but has not been formally proven to be true under the rules of mathematical logic.

Chapter 2. PERMUTATIONS, COSETS, AND DIRECT PRODUCTS

a. Conjecture0
b. Concept
c. Undefined
d. Undefined

48. _____ are objects, characters, or other concrete representations of ideas, concepts, or other abstractions.
   a. Thing
   b. Symbols0
   c. Undefined
   d. Undefined

49. _____ was a British mathematician. He helped found the modern British school of pure mathematics.
   a. Person
   b. Arthur Cayley0
   c. Undefined
   d. Undefined

50. _____ is that branch of mathematics concerned with the study of groups. These are sets with a rule, or operation. The operation in a group must satisfy closure and have these three additional properties: 1) The operation must have the property of associativity. 2) There must be an identity element. 3) Every element must have a corresponding inverse element. _____ is used throughout mathematics and has several applications in physics and chemistry. Groups can be finite or infinite. A classification of finite simple groups, completed in 1983, is one of the major achievements of mathematics in the 20th century.
   a. Group theory0
   b. Thing
   c. Undefined
   d. Undefined

51. In mathematics, a _____ is a countable collection of open covers of a topological space that satisfies certain separation axioms.
   a. Development0
   b. Thing
   c. Undefined
   d. Undefined

52. A _____ is a set whose members are members of another set or a set contained within another set.
   a. Thing
   b. Subset0
   c. Undefined
   d. Undefined

53. A _____, is a symbolized depiction of space which highlights relations between components of that space. Most usually a _____ is a two-dimensional, geometrically accurate representation of a three-dimensional space.
   a. Map0
   b. Thing
   c. Undefined
   d. Undefined

54. In mathematics, the notion of _____ is a generalization of the notion of invertible.
   a. Cancellation0
   b. Thing
   c. Undefined
   d. Undefined

55. The _____, the average in everyday English, which is also called the arithmetic _____ (and is distinguished from the geometric _____ or harmonic _____). The average is also called the sample _____. The expected value of a random variable, which is also called the population _____.
   a. Mean0
   b. Thing
   c. Undefined
   d. Undefined

56. A _____ is a simplified and structured visual representation of concepts, ideas, constructions, relations, statistical data, anatomy etc used in all aspects of human activities to visualize and clarify the topic.

Chapter 2. PERMUTATIONS, COSETS, AND DIRECT PRODUCTS

a. Thing
b. Diagram0
c. Undefined
d. Undefined

57. In mathematics, a _____ is a rectangular table of numbers or, more generally, a table consisting of abstract quantities that can be added and multiplied.
a. Thing
b. Matrix0
c. Undefined
d. Undefined

58. A _____ fraction is a fraction in which the absolute value of the numerator is less than the denominator--hence, the absolute value of the fraction is less than 1.
a. Thing
b. Proper0
c. Undefined
d. Undefined

59. The _____ is a unit of plane angle. It is represented by the symbol "rad" or, more rarely, by the superscript c (for "circular measure"). For example, an angle of 1.2 radians would be written "1.2 rad" or "1.2c" (second symbol can produce confusion with centigrads).
a. Thing
b. Radian0
c. Undefined
d. Undefined

60. In mathematics, a _____ (also spelled reflexion) is a map that transforms an object into its mirror image.
a. Concept
b. Reflection0
c. Undefined
d. Undefined

61. In physics, an _____ is the path that an object makes around another object while under the influence of a source of centripetal force, such as gravity.
a. Thing
b. Orbit0
c. Undefined
d. Undefined

62. An _____ is a binary relation between two elements of a set which groups them together as being equivalent in some way.
a. Thing
b. Equivalence relation0
c. Undefined
d. Undefined

63. Generally, a _____ is a splitting of something into parts.
a. Thing
b. Partition0
c. Undefined
d. Undefined

64. In set theory and its applications throughout mathematics, _____ are a collection of sets (or sometimes other mathematical objects) that can be unambiguously defined by a property that all its members share.
a. Classes0
b. Thing
c. Undefined
d. Undefined

65. _____ are groups whose members are members of another set or a set contained within another set.
a. Thing
b. Subsets0
c. Undefined
d. Undefined

Chapter 2. PERMUTATIONS, COSETS, AND DIRECT PRODUCTS

66. In botany, _____ are above-ground plant organs specialized for photosynthesis. Their characteristics are typically analyzed by using Fiobonacci's sequences.
    a. Thing
    b. Leaves0
    c. Undefined
    d. Undefined

67. The _____ are the only integral domain whose positive elements are well-ordered, and in which order is preserved by addition. Like the natural numbers, the _____ form a countably infinite set. The set of all _____ is usually denoted in mathematics by a boldface Z .
    a. Thing
    b. Integers0
    c. Undefined
    d. Undefined

68. In Euclidean geometry, a _____ is the set of all points in a plane at a fixed distance, called the radius, from a given point, the center.
    a. Thing
    b. Circle0
    c. Undefined
    d. Undefined

69. In mathematics, two sets are said to be _____ if they have no element in common. For example, {1, 2, 3} and {4, 5, 6} are sets which are _____.
    a. Thing
    b. Disjoint0
    c. Undefined
    d. Undefined

70. In mathematics, factorization (British English: factorisation) or factoring is the decomposition of an object (for example, a number, a polynomial, or a matrix) into a product of other objects, or _____, which when multiplied together give the original.
    a. Thing
    b. Factors0
    c. Undefined
    d. Undefined

71. In mathematics, a _____ is an ordered list of objects. Like a set, it contains members, also called elements or terms, and the number of terms is called the length of the _____. Unlike a set, order matters, and the exact same elements can appear multiple times at different positions in the _____.
    a. Thing
    b. Sequence0
    c. Undefined
    d. Undefined

72. In mathematics, the conjugate _____ or adjoint matrix of an m-by-n matrix A with complex entries is the n-by-m matrix A* obtained from A by taking the transpose and then taking the complex conjugate of each entry.
    a. Pairs0
    b. Thing
    c. Undefined
    d. Undefined

73. In informal language, a _____ is a function that swaps two elements of a set.
    a. Transposition0
    b. Thing
    c. Undefined
    d. Undefined

74. A _____ is a mathematical statement which follows easily from a previously proven statement, typically a mathematical theorem.

Chapter 2. PERMUTATIONS, COSETS, AND DIRECT PRODUCTS

a. Thing
b. Corollary0
c. Undefined
d. Undefined

75. In mathematics, an _____ (or neutral element) is a special type of element of a set with respect to a binary operation on that set.
   a. Identity element0
   b. Concept
   c. Undefined
   d. Undefined

76. In mathematics, a _____ of an integer n, also called a factor of n, is an integer which evenly divides n without leaving a remainder.
   a. Thing
   b. Divisor0
   c. Undefined
   d. Undefined

77. _____ is the state of being greater than any finite real or natural number, however large.
   a. Thing
   b. Infinite0
   c. Undefined
   d. Undefined

78. In mathematics, an _____, also called a commutative group, is a group such that a * b= b*a for all and b in G. In other words, the order in which the binary operation is performed doesnt matter.
   a. Abelian group0
   b. Thing
   c. Undefined
   d. Undefined

79. _____ is electromagnetic radiation with a wavelength that is visible to the eye (visible _____) or, in a technical or scientific context, electromagnetic radiation of any wavelength.
   a. Light0
   b. Thing
   c. Undefined
   d. Undefined

80. In common philosophical language, a proposition or _____, is the content of an assertion, that is, it is true-or-false and defined by the meaning of a particular piece of language.
   a. Statement0
   b. Concept
   c. Undefined
   d. Undefined

81. In mathematics, a _____ number (or a _____) is a natural number that has exactly two (distinct) natural number divisors, which are 1 and the _____ number itself.
   a. Thing
   b. Prime0
   c. Undefined
   d. Undefined

82. The word _____ is used in a variety of ways in mathematics.
   a. Thing
   b. Index0
   c. Undefined
   d. Undefined

83. _____ Logic is a concept in traditional logic referring to a "type of immediate inference in which from a given proposition another proposition is inferred which has as its subject the predicate of the original proposition and as its predicate the subject of the original proposition (the quality of the proposition being retained)."

Chapter 2. PERMUTATIONS, COSETS, AND DIRECT PRODUCTS

    a. Concept
    c. Undefined
    b. Converse0
    d. Undefined

84. _____ is a natural number that has exactly two distinct natural number divisors, which are 1 and the _____ itself.
    a. Thing
    c. Undefined
    b. Prime number0
    d. Undefined

85. _____ is a trigonemtric function that is important when studying triangles and modeling periodic phenomena, among other applications.
    a. Thing
    c. Undefined
    b. Sine0
    d. Undefined

86. In mathematics, a _____ may be described informally as a number that can be given by an infinite decimal representation.
    a. Thing
    c. Undefined
    b. Real number0
    d. Undefined

87. In mathematics, the _____ inverse, or opposite, of a number n is the number that, when added to n, yields zero. The _____ inverse of n is denoted −n.
    a. Thing
    c. Undefined
    b. Additive0
    d. Undefined

88. Leonhard _____ was a pioneering Swiss mathematician and physicist, who spent most of his life in Russia and Germany.
    a. Euler0
    c. Undefined
    b. Person
    d. Undefined

89. A _____ is the result of the addition of a set of numbers. The numbers may be natural numbers, complex numbers, matrices, or still more complicated objects. An infinite _____ is a subtle procedure known as a series.
    a. Sum0
    c. Undefined
    b. Thing
    d. Undefined

90. In group theory, a _____ or monogenous group is a group that can be generated by a single element, in the sense that the group has an element g called a "generator" of the group such that, when written multiplicatively, every element of the group is a power of g a multiple of g when the notation is additive.
    a. Cyclic group0
    c. Undefined
    b. Thing
    d. Undefined

91. _____ means of or relating to the French philosopher and mathematician René Descartes.
    a. Cartesian0
    c. Undefined
    b. Thing
    d. Undefined

92. In mathematics, the _____ is a direct product of sets. Specifically, the _____ of two sets X (for example the points on an x-axis) and Y (for example the points on a y-axis), denoted X × Y, is the set of all possible ordered pairs whose first component is a member of X and whose second component is a member of Y.

Chapter 2. PERMUTATIONS, COSETS, AND DIRECT PRODUCTS

a. Cartesian product0
b. Thing
c. Undefined
d. Undefined

93. _____ is a property that a binary operation can have.
a. Thing
b. Associative law0
c. Undefined
d. Undefined

94. In mathematics, in the field of group theory, a _____ of a group is a quasisimple subnormal subgroup.
a. Component0
b. Concept
c. Undefined
d. Undefined

95. A _____ of a number is the product of that number with any integer.
a. Multiple0
b. Thing
c. Undefined
d. Undefined

96. In abstract algebra, a _____ G is a subset S such that every element of G can be expressed as the product of finitely many elements of S and their inverses.
a. Thing
b. Generating set of a group0
c. Undefined
d. Undefined

97. The _____ of two integers is the smallest positive integer that is a multiple of both intergers.
a. Least common multiple0
b. Thing
c. Undefined
d. Undefined

98. In mathematics, science including computer science, linguistics and engineering, an _____ is, generally speaking, an independent variable or input to a function.
a. Argument0
b. Thing
c. Undefined
d. Undefined

99. _____ is the branch of pure mathematics concerned with the properties of numbers in general, and integers in particular, as well as the wider classes of problems that arise from their study.
a. Number theory0
b. Thing
c. Undefined
d. Undefined

100. Johann Carl Friedrich Gauss or _____ was a German mathematician and scientist of profound genius who contributed significantly to many fields, including number theory, analysis, differential geometry, geodesy, magnetism, astronomy, and optics.
a. Person
b. Carl Gauss0
c. Undefined
d. Undefined

101. In mathematics, a _____ is a homogeneous polynomial of degree two in a number of variables.
a. Thing
b. Quadratic form0
c. Undefined
d. Undefined

Chapter 2. PERMUTATIONS, COSETS, AND DIRECT PRODUCTS

102. In mathematics, a _____ is a number in the form of a + bi where a and b are real numbers, and i is the imaginary unit, with the property i 2 = −1. The real number a is called the real part of the _____, and the real number b is the imaginary part.
   a. Thing
   b. Complex number0
   c. Undefined
   d. Undefined

103. _____ is bother the congnitive process of transferring information from a particular subject , and a linguistic expression corresponding to such a process.
   a. Thing
   b. Analogy0
   c. Undefined
   d. Undefined

104. A _____ signifies a point or points of probability on a subject e.g., the _____ of creativity, which allows for the formation of rule or norm or law by interpretation of the phenomena events that can be created.
   a. Thing
   b. Principle0
   c. Undefined
   d. Undefined

105. A _____ decimal is a number whose decimal representation eventually becomes periodic (i.e. the same number sequence _____ indefinitely).
   a. Thing
   b. Repeating0
   c. Undefined
   d. Undefined

106. _____ is a branch of mathematics concerning the study of structure, relation and quantity.
   a. Concept
   b. Algebra0
   c. Undefined
   d. Undefined

107. In number theory, the _____ of arithmetic (or unique factorization theorem) states that every natural number greater than 1 can be written as a unique product of prime numbers.
   a. Fundamental theorem0
   b. Concept
   c. Undefined
   d. Undefined

108. In mathematics, a _____ is the end result of a division problem. It can also be expressed as the number of times the divisor divides into the dividend.
   a. Quotient0
   b. Thing
   c. Undefined
   d. Undefined

109. In abstract algebra, the term _____ refers to a number of concepts related to elements of finite order in groups and to the failure of modules to be free.
   a. Torsion0
   b. Thing
   c. Undefined
   d. Undefined

110. In the theory of abelian groups, the _____ A_T of an abelian group A is the subgroup of A consisting of all elements that have finite order. An abelian group A is called a torsion group if every element of A has finite order and is called torsion-free if every element of A except the identity is of infinite order.
   a. Torsion subgroup0
   b. Thing
   c. Undefined
   d. Undefined

Chapter 2. PERMUTATIONS, COSETS, AND DIRECT PRODUCTS

111. In mathematics, the _____ inverse of a number x, denoted 1/x or x^{-1}, is the number which, when multiplied by x, yields 1. The _____ inverse of x is also called the reciprocal of x.
 a. Multiplicative0
 b. Thing
 c. Undefined
 d. Undefined

112. In mathematics, a _____ is a constant multiplicative factor of a certain object. The object can be such things as a variable, a vector, a function, etc. For example, the _____ of $9x^2$ is 9.
 a. Coefficient0
 b. Thing
 c. Undefined
 d. Undefined

113. _____ refers to the reduction of the body of a formerly living organism into simpler forms of matter.
 a. Thing
 b. Decomposing0
 c. Undefined
 d. Undefined

114. A _____ consists either of a suggested explanation for a phenomenon or of a reasoned proposal suggesting a possible correlation between multiple phenomena.
 a. Thing
 b. Hypothesis0
 c. Undefined
 d. Undefined

115. An _____ is a combination of numbers, operators, grouping symbols and/or free variables and bound variables arranged in a meaningful way which can be evaluated..
 a. Expression0
 b. Thing
 c. Undefined
 d. Undefined

116. In mathematics, a _____ is a two-dimensional manifold or surface that is perfectly flat.
 a. Plane0
 b. Thing
 c. Undefined
 d. Undefined

117. In mathematics, an _____, isometric isomorphism or congruence mapping is a distance-preserving isomorphism between metric spaces.
 a. Thing
 b. Isometry0
 c. Undefined
 d. Undefined

118. In Euclidean geometry, a _____ is moving every point a constant distance in a specified direction.
 a. Translation0
 b. Concept
 c. Undefined
 d. Undefined

119. The _____ rule, also known as a slipstick, is a mechanical analog computer, consisting of at least two finely divided scales , most often a fixed outer pair and a movable inner one, with a sliding window called the cursor.
 a. Slide0
 b. Thing
 c. Undefined
 d. Undefined

120. A _____ ratio, also called, Lift-to-drag ratio, _____ number, or finesse, is an aviation term that refers to the distance an aircraft will move forward for any given amount of lost altitude .

Chapter 2. PERMUTATIONS, COSETS, AND DIRECT PRODUCTS

a. Thing
b. Glide0
c. Undefined
d. Undefined

121. In geometry, a _____ is a type of isometry of the Euclidean plane: the combination of a reflection in a line and a translation along that line.
  a. Glide reflection0
  b. Thing
  c. Undefined
  d. Undefined

122. In mathematics, the concept of a _____ tries to capture the intuitive idea of a geometrical one-dimensional and continuous object. A simple example is the circle.
  a. Curve0
  b. Thing
  c. Undefined
  d. Undefined

123. In geometry, the _____ or barycenter of an object X in n-dimensional space is the intersection of all hyperplanes that divide X into two parts of equal moment about the hyperplane
  a. Thing
  b. Centroid0
  c. Undefined
  d. Undefined

124. An _____ is a straight line around which a geometric figure can be rotated.
  a. Thing
  b. Axis0
  c. Undefined
  d. Undefined

125. The word _____ comes from the 15th Century Latin word discretus which means separate.
  a. Discrete0
  b. Thing
  c. Undefined
  d. Undefined

126. In geometry, the _____ of an object is a point in some sense in the middle of the object.
  a. Thing
  b. Center0
  c. Undefined
  d. Undefined

127. The _____ of a function is an extension of the concept of a sum, and are identified or found through the use of integration.
  a. Integral0
  b. Thing
  c. Undefined
  d. Undefined

128. In astronomy, geography, geometry and related sciences and contexts, a plane is said to be _____ at a given point if it is locally perpendicular to the gradient of the gravity field, i.e., with the direction of the gravitational force at that point.
  a. Horizontal0
  b. Thing
  c. Undefined
  d. Undefined

129. In physics and in _____ calculus, a spatial _____, or simply _____, is a concept characterized by a magnitude and a direction.
  a. Vector0
  b. Thing
  c. Undefined
  d. Undefined

130. A _____ is a polygon with six edges and six vertices.

Chapter 2. PERMUTATIONS, COSETS, AND DIRECT PRODUCTS

a. Thing
b. Hexagon0
c. Undefined
d. Undefined

131. A _____ is a four-sided plane figure that has two sets of opposite parallel sides.
a. Parallelogram0
b. Concept
c. Undefined
d. Undefined

132. In geometry, a _____ (or rhomb; plural rhombi) is a quadrilateral in which all of the sides are of equal length, i.e., it is an equilateral quadrangle.
a. Rhombus0
b. Thing
c. Undefined
d. Undefined

133. _____ is a set, with some particular properties and usually some additional structure, such as the operations of addition or multiplication, for instance.
a. Thing
b. Space0
c. Undefined
d. Undefined

134. A _____ (or shape) refers to the external two-dimensional outline, appearance or configuration of some thing - in contrast to the matter or content or substance of which it is composed.
a. Plane figure0
b. Thing
c. Undefined
d. Undefined

135. In mathematics, a _____ function in the sense of algebraic geometry is an everywhere-defined, polynomial function on an algebraic variety V with values in the field K over which V is defined.
a. Regular0
b. Thing
c. Undefined
d. Undefined

136. A _____ is a set of numbers that designate location in a given reference system, such as x,y in a planar _____ system or an x,y,z in a three-dimensional _____ system.
a. Coordinate0
b. Thing
c. Undefined
d. Undefined

137. An _____ is when two lines intersect somewhere on a plane creating a right angle at intersection
a. Thing
b. Axes0
c. Undefined
d. Undefined

138. In Euclidean geometry, a uniform _____ is a linear transformation that enlargers or diminishes objects, and whose _____ factor is the same in all directions. This is also called homothethy.
a. Thing
b. Scale0
c. Undefined
d. Undefined

139. In mathematics, an _____ number is a complex number whose square is a negative real number. They were defined in 1572 by Rafael Bombelli.
a. Imaginary0
b. Thing
c. Undefined
d. Undefined

Chapter 3. HOMOMORPHISMS AND FACTOR GROUPS

1. In mathematics, a _____ is a group which is not the trivial group and whose only normal subgroups are the trivial group and the group itself.
   a. Simple group0
   b. Thing
   c. Undefined
   d. Undefined

2. _____ is the mathematical action of repeatedly adding or subtracting one, usually to find out how many objects there are or to set aside a desired number of objects.
   a. Counting0
   b. Thing
   c. Undefined
   d. Undefined

3. A _____, is a symbolized depiction of space which highlights relations between components of that space. Most usually a _____ is a two-dimensional, geometrically accurate representation of a three-dimensional space.
   a. Map0
   b. Thing
   c. Undefined
   d. Undefined

4. In mathematics, a _____ is the result of multiplying, or an expression that identifies factors to be multiplied.
   a. Product0
   b. Thing
   c. Undefined
   d. Undefined

5. A _____ is a calculation involving two input quantities. It can be accomplished using either a binary function or binary operator.
   a. Binary operation0
   b. Thing
   c. Undefined
   d. Undefined

6. _____ is the rearrangement of objects or symbols into distinguishable sequences.
   a. Permutation0
   b. Thing
   c. Undefined
   d. Undefined

7. In informal language, a _____ is a function that swaps two elements of a set.
   a. Transposition0
   b. Thing
   c. Undefined
   d. Undefined

8. In mathematics, a _____ may be described informally as a number that can be given by an infinite decimal representation.
   a. Thing
   b. Real number0
   c. Undefined
   d. Undefined

9. In abstract algebra, a _____ is a structure-preserving map between two algebraic structures. The word _____ comes from the Greek language: homo meaning "same" and morphi meaning "shape".
   a. Thing
   b. Homomorphism0
   c. Undefined
   d. Undefined

10. The mathematical concept of a _____ expresses the intuitive idea of deterministic dependence between two quantities, one of which is viewed as primary and the other as secondary. A _____ then is a way to associate a unique output for each input of a specified type, for example, a real number or an element of a given set.

Chapter 3. HOMOMORPHISMS AND FACTOR GROUPS

a. Thing
b. Function0
c. Undefined
d. Undefined

11. In mathematics, the _____ inverse, or opposite, of a number n is the number that, when added to n, yields zero. The _____ inverse of n is denoted −n.
    a. Additive0
    b. Thing
    c. Undefined
    d. Undefined

12. A _____ is the result of the addition of a set of numbers. The numbers may be natural numbers, complex numbers, matrices, or still more complicated objects. An infinite _____ is a subtle procedure known as a series.
    a. Thing
    b. Sum0
    c. Undefined
    d. Undefined

13. In physics and in _____ calculus, a spatial _____, or simply _____, is a concept characterized by a magnitude and a direction.
    a. Thing
    b. Vector0
    c. Undefined
    d. Undefined

14. In mathematics, a matrix can be thought of as each row or _____ being a vector. Hence, a space formed by row vectors or _____ vectors are said to be a row space or a _____ space.
    a. Column0
    b. Concept
    c. Undefined
    d. Undefined

15. _____ is an m × 1 matrix, i.e. a matrix consisting of a single column of m elements.
    a. Column vector0
    b. Thing
    c. Undefined
    d. Undefined

16. In mathematics, in the field of group theory, a _____ of a group is a quasisimple subnormal subgroup.
    a. Component0
    b. Concept
    c. Undefined
    d. Undefined

17. In mathematics, the _____ inverse of a number x, denoted 1/x or x^{-1}, is the number which, when multiplied by x, yields 1. The _____ inverse of x is also called the reciprocal of x.
    a. Multiplicative0
    b. Thing
    c. Undefined
    d. Undefined

18. In mathematics, a _____ is a rectangular table of numbers or, more generally, a table consisting of abstract quantities that can be added and multiplied.
    a. Matrix0
    b. Thing
    c. Undefined
    d. Undefined

19. In mathematics, the idea of _____ generalises the concepts of negation, in relation to addition, and reciprocal, in relation to multiplication.
    a. Inverse element0
    b. Thing
    c. Undefined
    d. Undefined

Chapter 3. HOMOMORPHISMS AND FACTOR GROUPS

20. In algebra, a _____ is a function depending on n that associates a scalar, $det(A)$, to every $n \times n$ square matrix A.
   a. Thing
   b. Determinant0
   c. Undefined
   d. Undefined

21. The _____, the average in everyday English, which is also called the arithmetic _____ (and is distinguished from the geometric _____ or harmonic _____). The average is also called the sample _____. The expected value of a random variable, which is also called the population _____.
   a. Mean0
   b. Thing
   c. Undefined
   d. Undefined

22. A _____ function is a function for which, intuitively, small changes in the input result in small changes in the output.
   a. Continuous0
   b. Event
   c. Undefined
   d. Undefined

23. In mathematics, a _____ of a k-place relation $L \subseteq X_1 \times \ldots \times X_k$ is one of the sets X_j, $1 \le j \le k$. In the special case where k = 2 and $L \subseteq X_1 \times X_2$ is a function $L : X_1 \to X_2$, it is conventional to refer to X_1 as the _____ of the function and to refer to X_2 as the codomain of the function.
   a. Domain0
   b. Thing
   c. Undefined
   d. Undefined

24. In mathematics, computing, linguistics, and related disciplines, an _____ is a finite list of well-defined instructions for accomplishing some task which, given an initial state, will terminate in a defined end-state.
   a. Concept
   b. Algorithm0
   c. Undefined
   d. Undefined

25. The _____ is a theorem in mathematics which precisely expresses the outcome of the usual process of division of integers. The name is something of a misnomer, as it is a theorem, not an algorithm, i.e. a well-defined procedure for achieving a specific task — although the _____ can be used to find the greatest common divisor of two integers.
   a. Thing
   b. Division Algorithm0
   c. Undefined
   d. Undefined

26. A _____ is 360° or 2δ radians.
   a. Thing
   b. Turn0
   c. Undefined
   d. Undefined

27. In geographic information systems, a _____ comprises an entity with a geographic location, typically determined by points, arcs, or polygons. Carriageways and cadastres exemplify _____ data.
   a. Feature0
   b. Thing
   c. Undefined
   d. Undefined

28. In mathematics, _____ is a part of the set theoretic notion of function.
   a. Thing
   b. Image0
   c. Undefined
   d. Undefined

Chapter 3. HOMOMORPHISMS AND FACTOR GROUPS

29. In mathematics, the _____ of a function is the set of all "output" values produced by that function. Given a function $f : A \to B$, the _____ of f, is defined to be the set $\{x \in B : x = f(a) \text{ for some } a \in A\}$.
    a. Thing
    b. Range0
    c. Undefined
    d. Undefined

30. In mathematics, a _____ is a statement that can be proved on the basis of explicitly stated or previously agreed assumptions.
    a. Thing
    b. Theorem0
    c. Undefined
    d. Undefined

31. _____ element of an element x with respect to a binary operation * with identity element e is an element y such that $x * y = y * x = e$. In particular,
    a. Thing
    b. Inverse0
    c. Undefined
    d. Undefined

32. In mathematics, an _____ (Greek:isos "equal", and morphe "shape") is a bijective map f such that both f and its inverse f^{-1} are homomorphisms, i.e. *structure-preserving* mappings.
    a. Isomorphism0
    b. Thing
    c. Undefined
    d. Undefined

33. An _____ or member of a set is an object that when collected together make up the set.
    a. Thing
    b. Element0
    c. Undefined
    d. Undefined

34. In group theory, given a group G under a binary operation *, we say that some subset H of G is a _____ of G if H also forms a group under the operation *.
    a. Thing
    b. Subgroup0
    c. Undefined
    d. Undefined

35. An _____ is an equality that remains true regardless of the values of any variables that appear within it, to distinguish it from an equality which is true under more particular conditions.
    a. Identity0
    b. Thing
    c. Undefined
    d. Undefined

36. In mathematics, an _____ (or neutral element) is a special type of element of a set with respect to a binary operation on that set.
    a. Concept
    b. Identity element0
    c. Undefined
    d. Undefined

37. In mathematics, a _____ is a demonstration that, assuming certain axioms, some statement is necessarily true.
    a. Thing
    b. Proof0
    c. Undefined
    d. Undefined

38. In mathematics, the _____ , or members of a set or more generally a class are all those objects which when collected together make up the set or class.

Chapter 3. HOMOMORPHISMS AND FACTOR GROUPS

    a. Thing
    c. Undefined
    b. Elements0
    d. Undefined

39. In common philosophical language, a proposition or _____, is the content of an assertion, that is, it is true-or-false and defined by the meaning of a particular piece of language.
    a. Statement0
    c. Undefined
    b. Concept
    d. Undefined

40. In category theory and its applications to other branches of mathematics, _____ are a generalization of the kernels of group homomorphisms and the kernels of module homomorphisms and certain other kernels from algebra.
    a. Kernel0
    c. Undefined
    b. Thing
    d. Undefined

41. In mathematics, if G is a group, H a subgroup of G, and g an element of G, then, gH = {gh : h an element of H } is a left _____ of H in G, and Hg = {hg : h an element of H } is a right _____ of H in G.
    a. Coset0
    c. Undefined
    b. Thing
    d. Undefined

42. In geometry, a line _____ is a part of a line that is bounded by two end points, and contains every point on the line between its end points.
    a. Segment0
    c. Undefined
    b. Concept
    d. Undefined

43. In geometry, a _____ is defined as a quadrilateral where all four of its angles are right angles.
    a. Thing
    c. Undefined
    b. Rectangle0
    d. Undefined

44. In mathematics, _____ geometry was the traditional name for the geometry of three-dimensional Euclidean space — for practical purposes the kind of space we live in.
    a. Thing
    c. Undefined
    b. Solid0
    d. Undefined

45. In astronomy, geography, geometry and related sciences and contexts, a plane is said to be _____ at a given point if it is locally perpendicular to the gradient of the gravity field, i.e., with the direction of the gravitational force at that point.
    a. Thing
    c. Undefined
    b. Horizontal0
    d. Undefined

46. A _____ is a part of a line that is bounded by two end points, and contains every point on the line between its end points.
    a. Thing
    c. Undefined
    b. Line segment0
    d. Undefined

47. Generally, a _____ is a splitting of something into parts.
    a. Partition0
    c. Undefined
    b. Thing
    d. Undefined

Chapter 3. HOMOMORPHISMS AND FACTOR GROUPS

48. A _____ is a set whose members are members of another set or a set contained within another set.
    a. Subset0
    b. Thing
    c. Undefined
    d. Undefined

49. A _____ is a set of numbers that designate location in a given reference system, such as x,y in a planar _____ system or an x,y,z in a three-dimensional _____ system.
    a. Coordinate0
    b. Thing
    c. Undefined
    d. Undefined

50. In mathematics, the _____ of a coordinate system is the point where the axes of the system intersect.
    a. Thing
    b. Origin0
    c. Undefined
    d. Undefined

51. The _____ of a mathematical object is its size: a property by which it can be larger or smaller than other objects of the same kind; in technical terms, an ordering of the class of objects to which it belongs.
    a. Magnitude0
    b. Thing
    c. Undefined
    d. Undefined

52. In mathematics, a _____ is a two-dimensional manifold or surface that is perfectly flat.
    a. Plane0
    b. Thing
    c. Undefined
    d. Undefined

53. In mathematics, a _____ is a number in the form of a + bi where a and b are real numbers, and i is the imaginary unit, with the property i 2 = −1. The real number a is called the real part of the _____, and the real number b is the imaginary part.
    a. Thing
    b. Complex number0
    c. Undefined
    d. Undefined

54. In Euclidean geometry, a _____ is the set of all points in a plane at a fixed distance, called the radius, from a given point, the center.
    a. Circle0
    b. Thing
    c. Undefined
    d. Undefined

55. An _____ is a straight line around which a geometric figure can be rotated.
    a. Axis0
    b. Thing
    c. Undefined
    d. Undefined

56. In mathematics, the _____ of two sets A and B is the set that contains all elements of A that also belong to B (or equivalently, all elements of B that also belong to A), but no other elements.
    a. Thing
    b. Intersection0
    c. Undefined
    d. Undefined

57. In mathematics and the mathematical sciences, a _____ is a fixed, but possibly unspecified, value. This is in contrast to a variable, which is not fixed.

Chapter 3. HOMOMORPHISMS AND FACTOR GROUPS

a. Constant0
b. Thing
c. Undefined
d. Undefined

58. _____ is a function whose values do not vary and thus are constant.
   a. Thing
   b. Constant function0
   c. Undefined
   d. Undefined

59. Évariste _____ was a French mathematician born in Bourg-la-Reine.
   a. Person
   b. Galois0
   c. Undefined
   d. Undefined

60. A _____ fraction is a fraction in which the absolute value of the numerator is less than the denominator--hence, the absolute value of the fraction is less than 1.
   a. Thing
   b. Proper0
   c. Undefined
   d. Undefined

61. _____ refers to the reduction of the body of a formerly living organism into simpler forms of matter.
   a. Thing
   b. Decomposing0
   c. Undefined
   d. Undefined

62. In mathematics, a _____ of a complex-valued function f is a member x of the domain of f such that f(x) vanishes at x, that is, x : f (x) = 0.
   a. Thing
   b. Root0
   c. Undefined
   d. Undefined

63. Marie Ennemond _____ was a French mathematician, known both for his foundational work in group theory and for his influential Cours d'analyse. He was born in Lyon and educated at the École polytechnique. He was an engineer by profession; later in life he taught at the École polytechnique and the Collège de France; where he had a reputation for eccentric choices of notation.
   a. Camille Jordan0
   b. Thing
   c. Undefined
   d. Undefined

64. A _____ is a mathematical statement which follows easily from a previously proven statement, typically a mathematical theorem.
   a. Corollary0
   b. Thing
   c. Undefined
   d. Undefined

65. A _____ is a negotiable instrument instructing a financial institution to pay a specific amount of a specific currency from a specific demand account held in the maker/depositor's name with that institution. Both the maker and payee may be natural persons or legal entities.
   a. Thing
   b. Check0
   c. Undefined
   d. Undefined

66. In mathematics, a set is called _____ if there is a bijection between the set and some set of the form {1, 2, ..., n} where n is a natural number.

Chapter 3. HOMOMORPHISMS AND FACTOR GROUPS

a. Finite0
b. Thing
c. Undefined
d. Undefined

67. In mathematics, _____ is an elementary arithmetic operation. When one of the numbers is a whole number, _____ is the repeated sum of the other number.
   a. Thing
   b. Multiplication0
   c. Undefined
   d. Undefined

68. A _____ is the part of the dividend that is left over when the dividend is not evenly divisible by the divisor.
   a. Thing
   b. Remainder0
   c. Undefined
   d. Undefined

69. The _____ is a measurement of how a function changes when the values of its inputs change.
   a. Thing
   b. Derivative0
   c. Undefined
   d. Undefined

70. In linear algebra, the _____ of an n-by-n square matrix A is defined to be the sum of the elements on the main diagonal of A,
   a. Thing
   b. Trace0
   c. Undefined
   d. Undefined

71. In linear algebra, the _____ of a square matrix is the diagonal which runs from the top left corner to the bottom right corner.
   a. Thing
   b. Main diagonal0
   c. Undefined
   d. Undefined

72. A _____ can refer to a line joining two nonadjacent vertices of a polygon or polyhedron, or in some contexts any upward or downward sloping line. .
   a. Thing
   b. Diagonal0
   c. Undefined
   d. Undefined

73. _____ is the state of being greater than any finite real or natural number, however large.
   a. Thing
   b. Infinite0
   c. Undefined
   d. Undefined

74. In mathematics, a _____ of an integer n, also called a factor of n, is an integer which evenly divides n without leaving a remainder.
   a. Divisor0
   b. Thing
   c. Undefined
   d. Undefined

75. An _____ is a function which does the reverse of a given function.
   a. Thing
   b. Inverse function0
   c. Undefined
   d. Undefined

76. In set theory and its applications throughout mathematics, _____ are a collection of sets (or sometimes other mathematical objects) that can be unambiguously defined by a property that all its members share.

a. Thing
b. Classes0
c. Undefined
d. Undefined

77. The _____ are the only integral domain whose positive elements are well-ordered, and in which order is preserved by addition. Like the natural numbers, the _____ form a countably infinite set. The set of all _____ is usually denoted in mathematics by a boldface Z .
a. Thing
b. Integers0
c. Undefined
d. Undefined

78. In geometry, two sets are called _____ if one can be transformed into the other by an isometry, i.e., a combination of translations, rotations and reflections.
a. Thing
b. Congruent0
c. Undefined
d. Undefined

79. Mathematical _____ is used to represent ideas.
a. Thing
b. Notation0
c. Undefined
d. Undefined

80. In mathematics, _____ notation occurs when an author uses a mathematical notation in a way that is not formally correct but that seems likely to simplify the exposition .
a. Abuse of0
b. Thing
c. Undefined
d. Undefined

81. A _____ consists either of a suggested explanation for a phenomenon or of a reasoned proposal suggesting a possible correlation between multiple phenomena.
a. Thing
b. Hypothesis0
c. Undefined
d. Undefined

82. In mathematics, _____ is a property that a binary operation can have. Within an expression containing two or more of the same associative operators in a row, the order of operations does not matter as long as the sequence of the operands is not changed.
a. Associativity0
b. Thing
c. Undefined
d. Undefined

83. In mathematics, a _____ is the end result of a division problem. It can also be expressed as the number of times the divisor divides into the dividend.
a. Thing
b. Quotient0
c. Undefined
d. Undefined

84. In mathematics, an _____, also called a commutative group, is a group such that a * b= b*a for all and b in G. In other words, the order in which the binary operation is performed doesnt matter.
a. Abelian group0
b. Thing
c. Undefined
d. Undefined

85. A frame of _____ is a particular perspective from which the universe is observed.

Chapter 3. HOMOMORPHISMS AND FACTOR GROUPS

a. Thing
b. Reference0
c. Undefined
d. Undefined

86. The _____ integers are all the integers from zero on upwards.
a. Thing
b. Nonnegative0
c. Undefined
d. Undefined

87. In elementary algebra, an _____ is a set that contains every real number between two indicated numbers and may contain the two numbers themselves.
a. Thing
b. Interval0
c. Undefined
d. Undefined

88. In abstract algebra, the _____ relates the structure of two objects between which a homomorphism is given, and of the kernel and image of the homomorphism.
a. Thing
b. Fundamental homomorphism theorem0
c. Undefined
d. Undefined

89. In mathematics, an _____ is an isomorphism from a mathematical objct of itself while preserving all of its structure.
a. Automorphism0
b. Thing
c. Undefined
d. Undefined

90. In mathematics, an _____ is something that does not change under a set of transformations. The property of being an _____ is invariance.
a. Thing
b. Invariant0
c. Undefined
d. Undefined

91. In algebra, a _____ is a binomial formed by taking the opposite of the second term of a binomial.
a. Conjugate0
b. Thing
c. Undefined
d. Undefined

92. In abstract algebra, the term _____ refers to a number of concepts related to elements of finite order in groups and to the failure of modules to be free.
a. Thing
b. Torsion0
c. Undefined
d. Undefined

93. In group theory in mathematics, a _____ is a group in which each element has finite order. All finite groups are periodic. The concept of this group should not be confused with that of a cyclic group.
a. Thing
b. Periodic group0
c. Undefined
d. Undefined

94. In the theory of abelian groups, the _____ A_T of an abelian group A is the subgroup of A consisting of all elements that have finite order. An abelian group A is called a torsion group if every element of A has finite order and is called torsion-free if every element of A except the identity is of infinite order.

Chapter 3. HOMOMORPHISMS AND FACTOR GROUPS

    a. Torsion subgroup0   b. Thing
    c. Undefined   d. Undefined

95. An _____ is a binary relation between two elements of a set which groups them together as being equivalent in some way.
    a. Equivalence relation0   b. Thing
    c. Undefined   d. Undefined

96. In mathematics, the _____ gives an indication of the extent to which a certain binary operation fails to be commutative. There are different definitions used in group theory and ring theory.
    a. Commutator0   b. Thing
    c. Undefined   d. Undefined

97. In mathematics, a _____ of a positive integer n is a way of writing n as a sum of positive integers.
    a. Thing   b. Composition0
    c. Undefined   d. Undefined

98. In mathematics, a _____, formed by the composition of one function on another, represents the application of the former to the result of the application of the latter to the argument of the composite.
    a. Thing   b. Function composition0
    c. Undefined   d. Undefined

99. _____ are groups whose members are members of another set or a set contained within another set.
    a. Thing   b. Subsets0
    c. Undefined   d. Undefined

100. _____ Logic is a concept in traditional logic referring to a "type of immediate inference in which from a given proposition another proposition is inferred which has as its subject the predicate of the original proposition and as its predicate the subject of the original proposition (the quality of the proposition being retained)."
    a. Concept   b. Converse0
    c. Undefined   d. Undefined

101. In abstract algebra, a _____ G is a subset S such that every element of G can be expressed as the product of finitely many elements of S and their inverses.
    a. Thing   b. Generating set of a group0
    c. Undefined   d. Undefined

102. In mathematics and logic, a _____ proof is a way of showing the truth or falsehood of a given statement by a straightforward combination of established facts, usually existing lemmas and theorems, without making any further assumptions.
    a. Thing   b. Direct0
    c. Undefined   d. Undefined

103. In group theory, a _____ or monogenous group is a group that can be generated by a single element, in the sense that the group has an element g called a "generator" of the group such that, when written multiplicatively, every element of the group is a power of g a multiple of g when the notation is additive.

Chapter 3. HOMOMORPHISMS AND FACTOR GROUPS

a. Thing
c. Undefined
b. Cyclic group0
d. Undefined

104. _____ is a kind of property which exists as magnitude or multitude. It is among the basic classes of things along with quality, substance, change, and relation.
   a. Thing
   c. Undefined
   b. Amount0
   d. Undefined

105. _____ has many meanings, most of which simply .
   a. Power0
   c. Undefined
   b. Thing
   d. Undefined

106. Statistical _____ is a statistical procedure in which individual items are placed into groups based on quantitative information on one or more characteristics inherent in the items and based on a training set of previously labeled items.
   a. Thing
   c. Undefined
   b. Classification0
   d. Undefined

107. In mathematics, _____ is the decomposition of an object into a product of other objects, or factors, which when multiplied together give the original.
   a. Thing
   c. Undefined
   b. Factoring0
   d. Undefined

108. In mathematics, factorization (British English: factorisation) or factoring is the decomposition of an object (for example, a number, a polynomial, or a matrix) into a product of other objects, or _____, which when multiplied together give the original.
   a. Factors0
   c. Undefined
   b. Thing
   d. Undefined

109. In mathematics, a _____ number (or a _____) is a natural number that has exactly two (distinct) natural number divisors, which are 1 and the _____ number itself.
   a. Thing
   c. Undefined
   b. Prime0
   d. Undefined

110. _____ is that branch of mathematics concerned with the study of groups. These are sets with a rule, or operation. The operation in a group must satisfy closure and have these three additional properties: 1) The operation must have the property of associativity. 2) There must be an identity element. 3) Every element must have a corresponding inverse element. _____ is used throughout mathematics and has several applications in physics and chemistry. Groups can be finite or infinite. A classification of finite simple groups, completed in 1983, is one of the major achievements of mathematics in the 20th century.
   a. Thing
   c. Undefined
   b. Group theory0
   d. Undefined

111. In geometry, the _____ of an object is a point in some sense in the middle of the object.
   a. Center0
   c. Undefined
   b. Thing
   d. Undefined

Chapter 3. HOMOMORPHISMS AND FACTOR GROUPS

112. The word _____ is used in a variety of ways in mathematics.
   a. Index0
   b. Thing
   c. Undefined
   d. Undefined

113. Equivalence is the condition of being _____ or essentially equal.
   a. Equivalent0
   b. Thing
   c. Undefined
   d. Undefined

114. In mathematics, two sets are said to be _____ if they have no element in common. For example, {1, 2, 3} and {4, 5, 6} are sets which are _____.
   a. Thing
   b. Disjoint0
   c. Undefined
   d. Undefined

115. Two mathematical objects are equal if and only if they are precisely the same in every way. This defines a binary relation, _____, denoted by the sign of _____ "=" in such a way that the statement "x = y" means that x and y are equal.
   a. Thing
   b. Equality0
   c. Undefined
   d. Undefined

116. _____ is a collection of objects called vectors that, informally speaking, may be scaled and added.
   a. Vector space0
   b. Thing
   c. Undefined
   d. Undefined

117. _____ is a set, with some particular properties and usually some additional structure, such as the operations of addition or multiplication, for instance.
   a. Thing
   b. Space0
   c. Undefined
   d. Undefined

118. An _____ is any starting assumption from which other statements are logically derived
   a. Thing
   b. Axiom0
   c. Undefined
   d. Undefined

119. In linear algebra, real numbers are called scalars and relate to vectors in a vector space through the operation of _____ multiplication, in which a vector can be multiplied by a number to produce another vector.
   a. Scalar0
   b. Thing
   c. Undefined
   d. Undefined

120. A _____ is the sum of the elements of a sequence.
   a. Thing
   b. Series0
   c. Undefined
   d. Undefined

121. In geometry, a _____ is a special kind of point, usually a corner of a polygon, polyhedron, or higher dimensional polytope. In the geometry of curves a _____ is a point of where the first derivative of curvature is zero. In graph theory, a _____ is the fundamental unit out of which graphs are formed

Chapter 3. HOMOMORPHISMS AND FACTOR GROUPS

a. Thing
b. Vertex0
c. Undefined
d. Undefined

122. In plane geometry, a _____ is a polygon with four equal sides, four right angles, and parallel opposite sides. In algebra, the _____ of a number is that number multiplied by itself.
a. Square0
b. Thing
c. Undefined
d. Undefined

123. An _____ is when two lines intersect somewhere on a plane creating a right angle at intersection
a. Axes0
b. Thing
c. Undefined
d. Undefined

124. _____ is the middle point of a line segment.
a. Thing
b. Midpoint0
c. Undefined
d. Undefined

125. In physics, an _____ is the path that an object makes around another object while under the influence of a source of centripetal force, such as gravity.
a. Orbit0
b. Thing
c. Undefined
d. Undefined

126. The _____ is a unit of plane angle. It is represented by the symbol "rad" or, more rarely, by the superscript c (for "circular measure"). For example, an angle of 1.2 radians would be written "1.2 rad" or "1.2c" (second symbol can produce confusion with centigrads).
a. Thing
b. Radian0
c. Undefined
d. Undefined

127. In set theory and other branches of mathematics, the _____ of a collection of sets is the set that contains everything that belongs to any of the sets, but nothing else.
a. Thing
b. Union0
c. Undefined
d. Undefined

128. A _____ is a three-dimensional solid object bounded by six square faces, facets, or sides, with three meeting at each vertex.
a. Thing
b. Cube0
c. Undefined
d. Undefined

129. A _____ is a movement of an object in a circular motion. A two-dimensional object rotates around a center (or point) of _____. A three-dimensional object rotates around a line called an axis. If the axis of _____ is within the body, the body is said to rotate upon itself, or spinâ€"which implies relative speed and perhaps free-movement with angular momentum. A circular motion about an external point, e.g. the Earth about the Sun, is called an orbit or more properly an orbital revolution.
a. Thing
b. Rotation0
c. Undefined
d. Undefined

Chapter 3. HOMOMORPHISMS AND FACTOR GROUPS

130. _____ is a branch of pure mathematics concerning the study of discrete objects. It is related to many other areas of mathematics, such as algebra, probability theory, ergodic theory and geometry, as well as to applied subjects such as computer science and statistical physics.
   a. Thing
   b. Combinatorics0
   c. Undefined
   d. Undefined

131. In mathematics, the additive inverse, or _____ of a number n is the number that, when added to n, yields zero. The additive inverse of n is denoted −n. For example, 7 is −7, because 7 + (−7) = 0, and the additive inverse of −0.3 is 0.3, because −0.3 + 0.3 = 0.
   a. Opposite0
   b. Thing
   c. Undefined
   d. Undefined

132. In mathematics, the _____ of a number n is the number that, when added to n, yields zero. The _____ of n is denoted −n. For example, 7 is −7, because 7 + (−7) = 0, and the _____ of −0.3 is 0.3, because −0.3 + 0.3 = 0.
   a. Thing
   b. Additive inverse0
   c. Undefined
   d. Undefined

133. A _____ is one of the basic shapes of geometry: a polygon with three vertices and three sides which are straight line segments.
   a. Triangle0
   b. Thing
   c. Undefined
   d. Undefined

134. In mathematics, a _____ function in the sense of algebraic geometry is an everywhere-defined, polynomial function on an algebraic variety V with values in the field K over which V is defined.
   a. Regular0
   b. Thing
   c. Undefined
   d. Undefined

135. A _____ (plural: tetrahedra) is a polyhedron composed of four triangular faces, three of which meet at each vertex.
   a. Tetrahedron0
   b. Thing
   c. Undefined
   d. Undefined

136. _____ are of a number n in its third power-the result of multiplying it by itself three times.
   a. Thing
   b. Cubes0
   c. Undefined
   d. Undefined

137. In geometry, n-sided _____ are polyhedra made of an n-sided polygonal base, a translated copy, and n faces joining corresponding sides.
   a. Thing
   b. Prisms0
   c. Undefined
   d. Undefined

Chapter 4. RINGS AND FIELDS

1. In mathematics, a _____ is an algebraic structure in which addition and multiplication are defined and have properties listed below.
   - a. Ring0
   - b. Thing
   - c. Undefined
   - d. Undefined

2. A _____ is a calculation involving two input quantities. It can be accomplished using either a binary function or binary operator.
   - a. Thing
   - b. Binary operation0
   - c. Undefined
   - d. Undefined

3. The _____ relates to the binary operation of multiplication and addition.
   - a. Thing
   - b. Distributive law0
   - c. Undefined
   - d. Undefined

4. In mathematics, _____ is an elementary arithmetic operation. When one of the numbers is a whole number, _____ is the repeated sum of the other number.
   - a. Thing
   - b. Multiplication0
   - c. Undefined
   - d. Undefined

5. A _____ is a set whose members are members of another set or a set contained within another set.
   - a. Subset0
   - b. Thing
   - c. Undefined
   - d. Undefined

6. An _____ is any starting assumption from which other statements are logically derived
   - a. Axiom0
   - b. Thing
   - c. Undefined
   - d. Undefined

7. In mathematics, a _____ is a number in the form of a + bi where a and b are real numbers, and i is the imaginary unit, with the property i 2 = −1. The real number a is called the real part of the _____, and the real number b is the imaginary part.
   - a. Complex number0
   - b. Thing
   - c. Undefined
   - d. Undefined

8. A _____ is a symbolic representation denoting a quantity or expression. It often represents an "unknown" quantity that has the potential to change.
   - a. Variable0
   - b. Thing
   - c. Undefined
   - d. Undefined

9. In set theory and its applications throughout mathematics, _____ are a collection of sets (or sometimes other mathematical objects) that can be unambiguously defined by a property that all its members share.
   - a. Classes0
   - b. Thing
   - c. Undefined
   - d. Undefined

10. The _____ are the only integral domain whose positive elements are well-ordered, and in which order is preserved by addition. Like the natural numbers, the _____ form a countably infinite set. The set of all _____ is usually denoted in mathematics by a boldface Z .

a. Integers0
b. Thing
c. Undefined
d. Undefined

11. In mathematics, an _____ is a complex number that is an algebraic element over the rational numbers.
   a. Algebraic number0
   b. Thing
   c. Undefined
   d. Undefined

12. In mathematics, a _____ is an expression that is constructed from one or more variables and constants, using only the operations of addition, subtraction, multiplication, and constant positive whole number exponents. is a _____. Note in particular that division by an expression containing a variable is not in general allowed in polynomials. [1]
   a. Thing
   b. Polynomial0
   c. Undefined
   d. Undefined

13. In abstract algebra, a _____ is the set of polynomials in one or more variables with coefficients in a ring.
   a. Polynomial ring0
   b. Thing
   c. Undefined
   d. Undefined

14. _____ was a German mathematician, recognized as one of the most influential and universal mathematicians of the 19th and early 20th centuries. He invented or developed a broad range of fundamental ideas, in invariant theory, the axiomatization of geometry, and with the notion of Hilbert space, one of the foundations of functional analysis.
   a. David Hilbert0
   b. Person
   c. Undefined
   d. Undefined

15. _____ was a German-born Jewish mathematician. Along with Emil Artin and Helmut Hasse, she founded the theory of central simple algebras.
   a. Person
   b. Emmy Noether0
   c. Undefined
   d. Undefined

16. A _____ is a ring in which the multiplication operation obeys the commutative law.
   a. Commutative ring0
   b. Thing
   c. Undefined
   d. Undefined

17. The _____ are finiteness properties statisfied by certain algebraic structures, most importantly, ideals in a commutatice rings inthe works of David Hilbert, Emmy Nöther, and Emil Artin.
   a. Ascending chain condition0
   b. Thing
   c. Undefined
   d. Undefined

18. An _____ or member of a set is an object that when collected together make up the set.
   a. Thing
   b. Element0
   c. Undefined
   d. Undefined

19. In abstract algebra, a _____ G is a subset S such that every element of G can be expressed as the product of finitely many elements of S and their inverses.
   a. Generating set of a group0
   b. Thing
   c. Undefined
   d. Undefined

Chapter 4. RINGS AND FIELDS

20. In mathematics, science including computer science, linguistics and engineering, an _____ is, generally speaking, an independent variable or input to a function.
    a. Argument0
    b. Thing
    c. Undefined
    d. Undefined

21. In mathematics, _____ is a property that a binary operation can have. Within an expression containing two or more of the same associative operators in a row, the order of operations does not matter as long as the sequence of the operands is not changed.
    a. Thing
    b. Associativity0
    c. Undefined
    d. Undefined

22. In mathematics, a _____ is a rectangular table of numbers or, more generally, a table consisting of abstract quantities that can be added and multiplied.
    a. Matrix0
    b. Thing
    c. Undefined
    d. Undefined

23. A _____ is a deliberate process for transforming one or more inputs into one or more results.
    a. Calculation0
    b. Thing
    c. Undefined
    d. Undefined

24. Mathematical _____ is used to represent ideas.
    a. Notation0
    b. Thing
    c. Undefined
    d. Undefined

25. A _____ number is a positive integer which has a positive divisor other than one or itself.
    a. Thing
    b. Composite0
    c. Undefined
    d. Undefined

26. A _____, formed by the composition of one function on another, represents the application of the former to the result of the application of the latter to the argument of the composite.
    a. Composite function0
    b. Thing
    c. Undefined
    d. Undefined

27. In mathematics, a _____ of a positive integer n is a way of writing n as a sum of positive integers.
    a. Thing
    b. Composition0
    c. Undefined
    d. Undefined

28. The mathematical concept of a _____ expresses the intuitive idea of deterministic dependence between two quantities, one of which is viewed as primary and the other as secondary. A _____ then is a way to associate a unique output for each input of a specified type, for example, a real number or an element of a given set.
    a. Function0
    b. Thing
    c. Undefined
    d. Undefined

29. In mathematics, a _____, formed by the composition of one function on another, represents the application of the former to the result of the application of the latter to the argument of the composite.

Chapter 4. RINGS AND FIELDS

a. Thing
c. Undefined
b. Function composition0
d. Undefined

30. A _____ of a number is the product of that number with any integer.
    a. Thing
    c. Undefined
    b. Multiple0
    d. Undefined

31. _____ is that branch of mathematics concerned with the study of groups. These are sets with a rule, or operation. The operation in a group must satisfy closure and have these three additional properties: 1) The operation must have the property of associativity. 2) There must be an identity element. 3) Every element must have a corresponding inverse element. _____ is used throughout mathematics and has several applications in physics and chemistry. Groups can be finite or infinite. A classification of finite simple groups, completed in 1983, is one of the major achievements of mathematics in the 20th century.
    a. Group theory0
    c. Undefined
    b. Thing
    d. Undefined

32. In group theory, given a group G under a binary operation *, we say that some subset H of G is a _____ of G if H also forms a group under the operation *.
    a. Subgroup0
    c. Undefined
    b. Thing
    d. Undefined

33. In mathematics, in the field of group theory, a _____ of a group is a quasisimple subnormal subgroup.
    a. Concept
    c. Undefined
    b. Component0
    d. Undefined

34. In mathematics, a _____ is the result of multiplying, or an expression that identifies factors to be multiplied.
    a. Thing
    c. Undefined
    b. Product0
    d. Undefined

35. In mathematics and logic, a _____ proof is a way of showing the truth or falsehood of a given statement by a straightforward combination of established facts, usually existing lemmas and theorems, without making any further assumptions.
    a. Direct0
    c. Undefined
    b. Thing
    d. Undefined

36. An _____ is an equality that remains true regardless of the values of any variables that appear within it, to distinguish it from an equality which is true under more particular conditions.
    a. Identity0
    c. Undefined
    b. Thing
    d. Undefined

37. In mathematics, the _____ inverse, or opposite, of a number n is the number that, when added to n, yields zero. The _____ inverse of n is denoted −n.
    a. Additive0
    c. Undefined
    b. Thing
    d. Undefined

Chapter 4. RINGS AND FIELDS

38. In mathematics the _____ of a set which is equipped with the operation of addition is an element which, when added to any other element x in the set, yields x.
   a. Additive identity0
   b. Concept
   c. Undefined
   d. Undefined

39. _____ element of an element x with respect to a binary operation * with identity element e is an element y such that x * y = y * x = e. In particular,
   a. Thing
   b. Inverse0
   c. Undefined
   d. Undefined

40. In mathematics, the _____ of a number n is the number that, when added to n, yields zero. The _____ of n is denoted −n. For example, 7 is −7, because 7 + (−7) = 0, and the _____ of −0.3 is 0.3, because −0.3 + 0.3 = 0.
   a. Thing
   b. Additive inverse0
   c. Undefined
   d. Undefined

41. In mathematics, a _____ is a statement that can be proved on the basis of explicitly stated or previously agreed assumptions.
   a. Thing
   b. Theorem0
   c. Undefined
   d. Undefined

42. In mathematics, a _____ is a demonstration that, assuming certain axioms, some statement is necessarily true.
   a. Proof0
   b. Thing
   c. Undefined
   d. Undefined

43. In mathematics, the notion of _____ is a generalization of the notion of invertible.
   a. Thing
   b. Cancellation0
   c. Undefined
   d. Undefined

44. In statistics, a _____ measure is one which is measuring what is supposed to measure.
   a. Valid0
   b. Thing
   c. Undefined
   d. Undefined

45. In abstract algebra, a _____ is a structure-preserving map between two algebraic structures. The word _____ comes from the Greek language: homo meaning "same" and morphi meaning "shape".
   a. Thing
   b. Homomorphism0
   c. Undefined
   d. Undefined

46. In mathematics, the _____ inverse of a number x, denoted 1/x or x^{-1}, is the number which, when multiplied by x, yields 1. The _____ inverse of x is also called the reciprocal of x.
   a. Thing
   b. Multiplicative0
   c. Undefined
   d. Undefined

47. In mathematics, computing, linguistics, and related disciplines, an _____ is a finite list of well-defined instructions for accomplishing some task which, given an initial state, will terminate in a defined end-state.

a. Algorithm0
b. Concept
c. Undefined
d. Undefined

48. The _____ is a theorem in mathematics which precisely expresses the outcome of the usual process of division of integers. The name is something of a misnomer, as it is a theorem, not an algorithm, i.e. a well-defined procedure for achieving a specific task — although the _____ can be used to find the greatest common divisor of two integers.
    a. Division Algorithm0
    b. Thing
    c. Undefined
    d. Undefined

49. _____ is a branch of mathematics concerning the study of structure, relation and quantity.
    a. Algebra0
    b. Concept
    c. Undefined
    d. Undefined

50. In mathematics, an _____ (Greek:isos "equal", and morphe "shape") is a bijective map f such that both f and its inverse f^{-1} are homomorphisms, i.e. *structure-preserving* mappings.
    a. Isomorphism0
    b. Thing
    c. Undefined
    d. Undefined

51. An _____ is a binary relation between two elements of a set which groups them together as being equivalent in some way.
    a. Thing
    b. Equivalence relation0
    c. Undefined
    d. Undefined

52. In mathematics, an _____ (or neutral element) is a special type of element of a set with respect to a binary operation on that set.
    a. Concept
    b. Identity element0
    c. Undefined
    d. Undefined

53. In mathematics, an _____, also called a commutative group, is a group such that a * b= b*a for all and b in G. In other words, the order in which the binary operation is performed doesnt matter.
    a. Thing
    b. Abelian group0
    c. Undefined
    d. Undefined

54. In mathematics, the _____ of a number x, denoted 1/x or x^{-1}, is the number which, when multiplied by x, yields 1. The _____ of x is also called the reciprocal of x.
    a. Multiplicative inverse0
    b. Thing
    c. Undefined
    d. Undefined

55. In mathematics, the _____, or members of a set or more generally a class are all those objects which when collected together make up the set or class.
    a. Elements0
    b. Thing
    c. Undefined
    d. Undefined

56. _____ is the study of terms and their use — of words and compound words that are used in specific contexts.

Chapter 4. RINGS AND FIELDS

a. Terminology0
b. Thing
c. Undefined
d. Undefined

57. The _____ of measurement are a globally standardized and modernized form of the metric system.
a. Thing
b. Units0
c. Undefined
d. Undefined

58. _____ is the largest positive integer that divides both numbers without remainder.
a. Thing
b. Common Factor0
c. Undefined
d. Undefined

59. In mathematics, a _____ of a k-place relation $L \subseteq X_1 \times ... \times X_k$ is one of the sets X_j, $1 \leq j \leq k$. In the special case where k = 2 and $L \subseteq X_1 \times X_2$ is a function $L : X_1 \to X_2$, it is conventional to refer to X_1 as the _____ of the function and to refer to X_2 as the codomain of the function.
a. Domain0
b. Thing
c. Undefined
d. Undefined

60. In mathematics, a _____ may be described informally as a number that can be given by an infinite decimal representation.
a. Thing
b. Real number0
c. Undefined
d. Undefined

61. Julius Wilhelm Richard _____ (October 6, 1831 – February 12, 1916) was a German mathematician who did important work in abstract algebra, algebraic number theory and the foundations of the real numbers.
a. Dedekind0
b. Person
c. Undefined
d. Undefined

62. In logic, and especially in its applications to mathematics and philosophy, a _____ is an exception to a proposed general rule, i.e., a specific instance of the falsity of a universal quantification (a "for all" statement).
a. Thing
b. Counterexample0
c. Undefined
d. Undefined

63. In a mathematical proof or a syllogism, a _____ is a statement that is the logical consequence of preceding statements.
a. Concept
b. Conclusion0
c. Undefined
d. Undefined

64. In mathematics, _____ is the decomposition of an object into a product of other objects, or factors, which when multiplied together give the original.
a. Thing
b. Factoring0
c. Undefined
d. Undefined

65. The _____ of a mathematical object is its size: a property by which it can be larger or smaller than other objects of the same kind; in technical terms, an ordering of the class of objects to which it belongs.

a. Magnitude0
b. Thing
c. Undefined
d. Undefined

66. In mathematics, a _____ number (or a _____) is a natural number that has exactly two (distinct) natural number divisors, which are 1 and the _____ number itself.
   a. Prime0
   b. Thing
   c. Undefined
   d. Undefined

67. _____ is a mathematical operation, written a^n, involving two numbers, the base a and the exponent n.
   a. Exponentiation0
   b. Thing
   c. Undefined
   d. Undefined

68. An _____ of a product of sums expresses it as a sum of products by using the fact that multiplication distributes over addition.
   a. Thing
   b. Expansion0
   c. Undefined
   d. Undefined

69. In elementary algebra, a _____ is a polynomial with two terms: the sum of two monomials. It is the simplest kind of polynomial except for a monomial.
   a. Binomial0
   b. Thing
   c. Undefined
   d. Undefined

70. In mathematics and computer science, the concept of _____ arises in a number of places in abstract algebra; in particular, in the theory of projectors, closure operators and functional programming, in which it is connected to the property of referential transparency.
   a. Idempotence0
   b. Thing
   c. Undefined
   d. Undefined

71. In mathematics, an element x of a ring R is called _____ if there exists some positive integer n such that $x^n = 0$.
   a. Thing
   b. Nilpotent0
   c. Undefined
   d. Undefined

72. In mathematics, the _____ of two sets A and B is the set that contains all elements of A that also belong to B (or equivalently, all elements of B that also belong to A), but no other elements.
   a. Intersection0
   b. Thing
   c. Undefined
   d. Undefined

73. The _____ of a function is an extension of the concept of a sum, and are identified or found through the use of integration.
   a. Thing
   b. Integral0
   c. Undefined
   d. Undefined

74. A _____ is the part of the dividend that is left over when the dividend is not evenly divisible by the divisor.
   a. Remainder0
   b. Thing
   c. Undefined
   d. Undefined

Chapter 4. RINGS AND FIELDS

75. _____ in algebra is an application of polynomial long division.
    a. Remainder theorem0
    b. Thing
    c. Undefined
    d. Undefined

76. As an abstract term, _____ means similarity between objects.
    a. Congruence0
    b. Thing
    c. Undefined
    d. Undefined

77. In mathematics, factorization (British English: factorisation) or factoring is the decomposition of an object (for example, a number, a polynomial, or a matrix) into a product of other objects, or _____, which when multiplied together give the original.
    a. Factors0
    b. Thing
    c. Undefined
    d. Undefined

78. The _____ is a rule which states that when you add or multiply numbers, changing the order doesn't change the result.
    a. Thing
    b. Commutative law0
    c. Undefined
    d. Undefined

79. In mathematics, a _____ R is a ring for whick $x^2=x$ for all x in R; that is, R consists only of idempotent element. These rigns arise form Boolean algebra
    a. Boolean ring0
    b. Thing
    c. Undefined
    d. Undefined

80. _____ are groups whose members are members of another set or a set contained within another set.
    a. Subsets0
    b. Thing
    c. Undefined
    d. Undefined

81. _____ is a set of numbers, in the broadest sense of the word, together with one or more operations, such as addition or multiplication.
    a. Thing
    b. Number system0
    c. Undefined
    d. Undefined

82. In mathematics, a _____ of an integer n, also called a factor of n, is an integer which evenly divides n without leaving a remainder.
    a. Thing
    b. Divisor0
    c. Undefined
    d. Undefined

83. In mathematics, a _____ is the end result of a division problem. It can also be expressed as the number of times the divisor divides into the dividend.
    a. Thing
    b. Quotient0
    c. Undefined
    d. Undefined

84. In abstract algebra, a branch of mathematics, an _____ is a commutative ring with an additive identity 0 and a multiplicative identity 1 such that 0 ≠ 1, in which the product of any two non-zero elements is always non-zero.

a. Integral domain0 b. Thing
c. Undefined d. Undefined

85. In mathematics, a _____ is a constant multiplicative factor of a certain object. The object can be such things as a variable, a vector, a function, etc. For example, the _____ of $9x^2$ is 9.
   a. Coefficient0 b. Thing
   c. Undefined d. Undefined

86. In mathematics, a _____ is a preorder, i.e. an ordered set.
   a. Thing b. Hierarchy0
   c. Undefined d. Undefined

87. The word _____ comes from the Latin word linearis, which means created by lines.
   a. Thing b. Linear0
   c. Undefined d. Undefined

88. _____ is the mathematical action of repeatedly adding or subtracting one, usually to find out how many objects there are or to set aside a desired number of objects.
   a. Thing b. Counting0
   c. Undefined d. Undefined

89. In mathematics, a set is called _____ if there is a bijection between the set and some set of the form {1, 2, ..., n} where n is a natural number.
   a. Finite0 b. Thing
   c. Undefined d. Undefined

90. A _____ is a mathematical statement which follows easily from a previously proven statement, typically a mathematical theorem.
   a. Thing b. Corollary0
   c. Undefined d. Undefined

91. In linear algebra, two vectors in an inner product space are _____ if they are orthogonal (their inner product is 0) and both of unit length (the norm of each is 1). A set of vectors which is pairwise _____ (any two vectors in it are _____) is called an _____ set. A basis which forms an _____ set is called an _____ basis.
   a. Orthonormal0 b. Thing
   c. Undefined d. Undefined

92. The _____ of a ring R is defined to be the smallest positive integer n such that n a = 0, for all a in R.
   a. Thing b. Characteristic0
   c. Undefined d. Undefined

93. In mathematics, if G is a group, H a subgroup of G, and g an element of G, then, gH = {gh : h an element of H} is a left _____ of H in G, and Hg = {hg : h an element of H } is a right _____ of H in G.
   a. Thing b. Coset0
   c. Undefined d. Undefined

Chapter 4. RINGS AND FIELDS

94. _____, also known as _____ of Alexandria, was a Greek mathematician. His Elements is the most successful textbook in the history of mathematics. In it, the principles of geometry are deduced from a small set of axioms. His method of proving mathematical theorems by logical reasoning from accepted first principles remains the backbone of mathematics and is responsible for the field's characteristic rigor
   a. Euclid0
   b. Person
   c. Undefined
   d. Undefined

95. _____ the expected value of a random variable displays the average or central value of the variable. It is a summary value of the distribution of the variable.
   a. Thing
   b. Determining0
   c. Undefined
   d. Undefined

96. The _____, the average in everyday English, which is also called the arithmetic _____ (and is distinguished from the geometric _____ or harmonic _____). The average is also called the sample _____. The expected value of a random variable, which is also called the population _____.
   a. Mean0
   b. Thing
   c. Undefined
   d. Undefined

97. Leonhard _____ was a pioneering Swiss mathematician and physicist, who spent most of his life in Russia and Germany.
   a. Euler0
   b. Person
   c. Undefined
   d. Undefined

98. Compass and straightedge or ruler-and-compass _____ is the _____ of lengths or angles using only an idealized ruler and compass.
   a. Thing
   b. Construction0
   c. Undefined
   d. Undefined

99. In geometry, two sets are called _____ if one can be transformed into the other by an isometry, i.e., a combination of translations, rotations and reflections.
   a. Thing
   b. Congruent0
   c. Undefined
   d. Undefined

100. A _____ is a negotiable instrument instructing a financial institution to pay a specific amount of a specific currency from a specific demand account held in the maker/depositor's name with that institution. Both the maker and payee may be natural persons or legal entities.
   a. Check0
   b. Thing
   c. Undefined
   d. Undefined

101. An _____ is a collection of two not necessarily distinct objects, one of which is distinguished as the first coordinate and the other as the second coordinate.
   a. Thing
   b. Ordered pair0
   c. Undefined
   d. Undefined

102. _____ means of or relating to the French philosopher and mathematician René Descartes.

Chapter 4. RINGS AND FIELDS

a. Cartesian0
b. Thing
c. Undefined
d. Undefined

103. In mathematics, the _____ is a direct product of sets. Specifically, the _____ of two sets X (for example the points on an x-axis) and Y (for example the points on a y-axis), denoted X × Y, is the set of all possible ordered pairs whose first component is a member of X and whose second component is a member of Y.
   a. Thing
   b. Cartesian product0
   c. Undefined
   d. Undefined

104. In mathematics, a _____ number is a number which can be expressed as a ratio of two integers. Non-integer _____ numbers (commonly called fractions) are usually written as the vulgar fraction a / b, where b is not zero.
   a. Rational0
   b. Thing
   c. Undefined
   d. Undefined

105. In mathematics, the conjugate _____ or adjoint matrix of an m-by-n matrix A with complex entries is the n-by-m matrix A* obtained from A by taking the transpose and then taking the complex conjugate of each entry.
   a. Pairs0
   b. Thing
   c. Undefined
   d. Undefined

106. Equivalence is the condition of being _____ or essentially equal.
   a. Equivalent0
   b. Thing
   c. Undefined
   d. Undefined

107. Two mathematical objects are equal if and only if they are precisely the same in every way. This defines a binary relation, _____, denoted by the sign of _____ "=" in such a way that the statement "x = y" means that x and y are equal.
   a. Equality0
   b. Thing
   c. Undefined
   d. Undefined

108. An _____ is a combination of numbers, operators, grouping symbols and/or free variables and bound variables arranged in a meaningful way which can be evaluated..
   a. Expression0
   b. Thing
   c. Undefined
   d. Undefined

109. The _____ (symbol _____) and the millibar (symbol mbar, also mb) are units of pressure.
   a. Thing
   b. Bar0
   c. Undefined
   d. Undefined

110. A _____ is the part of a fraction that tells how many equal parts make up a whole, and which is used in the name of the fraction: "halves", "thirds", "fourths" or "quarters", "fifths" and so on.
   a. Denominator0
   b. Concept
   c. Undefined
   d. Undefined

111. A frame of _____ is a particular perspective from which the universe is observed.

Chapter 4. RINGS AND FIELDS

a. Thing
b. Reference0
c. Undefined
d. Undefined

112. In mathematics, there are several meanings of _____ depending on the subject.
a. Thing
b. Degree0
c. Undefined
d. Undefined

113. The _____ is the maximum of the degrees of all terms in the polynomial.
a. Thing
b. Degree of a polynomial0
c. Undefined
d. Undefined

114. _____ was a highly influential French philosopher, mathematician, scientist, and writer. Dubbed the "Founder of Modern Philosophy", and the "Father of Modern Mathematics". His theories provided the basis for the calculus of Newton and Leibniz, by applying infinitesimal calculus to the tangent line problem, thus permitting the evolution of that branch of modern mathematics
a. Descartes0
b. Person
c. Undefined
d. Undefined

115. _____ is the level of functional and/or metabolic efficiency of an organism at both the micro level.
a. Thing
b. Health0
c. Undefined
d. Undefined

116. There are two main approaches to _____ in mathematics. They are the model theory of _____ and the proof theory of _____.
a. Truth0
b. Thing
c. Undefined
d. Undefined

117. A _____ signifies a point or points of probability on a subject e.g., the _____ of creativity, which allows for the formation of rule or norm or law by interpretation of the phenomena events that can be created.
a. Thing
b. Principle0
c. Undefined
d. Undefined

118. A _____ fraction is a fraction in which the absolute value of the numerator is less than the denominator--hence, the absolute value of the fraction is less than 1.
a. Thing
b. Proper0
c. Undefined
d. Undefined

119. _____ is a trigonemtric function that is important when studying triangles and modeling periodic phenomena, among other applications.
a. Thing
b. Sine0
c. Undefined
d. Undefined

120. The deductive-nomological model is a formalized view of scientific _____ in natural language.
a. Thing
b. Explanation0
c. Undefined
d. Undefined

Chapter 4. RINGS AND FIELDS

121. _____ is electromagnetic radiation with a wavelength that is visible to the eye (visible _____) or, in a technical or scientific context, electromagnetic radiation of any wavelength.
- a. Light0
- b. Thing
- c. Undefined
- d. Undefined

122. A _____ is the result of the addition of a set of numbers. The numbers may be natural numbers, complex numbers, matrices, or still more complicated objects. An infinite _____ is a subtle procedure known as a series.
- a. Sum0
- b. Thing
- c. Undefined
- d. Undefined

123. _____ is the state of being greater than any finite real or natural number, however large.
- a. Thing
- b. Infinite0
- c. Undefined
- d. Undefined

124. _____ is a property that a binary operation can have.
- a. Thing
- b. Associative law0
- c. Undefined
- d. Undefined

125. In common philosophical language, a proposition or _____, is the content of an assertion, that is, it is true-or-false and defined by the meaning of a particular piece of language.
- a. Statement0
- b. Concept
- c. Undefined
- d. Undefined

126. In plane geometry, a _____ is a polygon with four equal sides, four right angles, and parallel opposite sides. In algebra, the _____ of a number is that number multiplied by itself.
- a. Square0
- b. Thing
- c. Undefined
- d. Undefined

127. In mathematics, a _____ is a polynomial equation of the second degree. The general form is $ax^2 + bx + c = 0$.
- a. Quadratic equation0
- b. Thing
- c. Undefined
- d. Undefined

128. A quadratic equation with real solutions, called roots, which may be real or complex, is given by the _____: $x = \frac{-b \pm \sqrt{b^2 - 4ac}}{2a}$.
- a. Thing
- b. Quadratic formula0
- c. Undefined
- d. Undefined

129. A _____ was a citizen of Babylonia, named for its capital city, Babylon, which was an ancient state in the south part of Mesopotamia (in modern Iraq), combining the territories of Sumer and Akkad.
- a. Place
- b. Babylonian0
- c. Undefined
- d. Undefined

130. In mathematics, a _____ of a number x is a number r such that $r^2 = x$, or in words, a number r whose square (the result of multiplying the number by itself) is x.

Chapter 4. RINGS AND FIELDS

a. Thing
c. Undefined
b. Square root0
d. Undefined

131. In mathematics, a _____ of a complex-valued function f is a member x of the domain of f such that f(x) vanishes at x, that is, x : f (x) = 0.
a. Root0
c. Undefined
b. Thing
d. Undefined

132. In mathematics, an _____ number is any real number that is not a rational number- that is, it is a number which cannot be expressed as a fraction m/n, where m and n are integers.
a. Irrational0
c. Undefined
b. Thing
d. Undefined

133. In mathematics, a _____ is a polynomial equation of the third degree.
a. Thing
c. Undefined
b. Cubic equation0
d. Undefined

134. _____ is a mathematical subject that includes the study of limits, derivatives, integrals, and power series and constitutes a major part of modern university curriculum.
a. Calculus0
c. Undefined
b. Thing
d. Undefined

135. In mathematics, a _____ section is a curve that can be formed by intersecting a cone with a plane.
a. Conic0
c. Undefined
b. Thing
d. Undefined

136. A _____ is a number that is less than zero.
a. Thing
c. Undefined
b. Negative number0
d. Undefined

137. In Euclidean geometry, a _____ is the set of all points in a plane at a fixed distance, called the radius, from a given point, the center.
a. Circle0
c. Undefined
b. Thing
d. Undefined

138. _____ is a kind of property which exists as magnitude or multitude. It is among the basic classes of things along with quality, substance, change, and relation.
a. Thing
c. Undefined
b. Amount0
d. Undefined

139. In mathematics, an _____ number is a complex number whose square is a negative real number. They were defined in 1572 by Rafael Bombelli.
a. Thing
c. Undefined
b. Imaginary0
d. Undefined

Chapter 4. RINGS AND FIELDS

140. In mathematics, a _____ is a countable collection of open covers of a topological space that satisfies certain separation axioms.
   a. Development0
   b. Thing
   c. Undefined
   d. Undefined

141. In arithmetic, _____ is a procedure for calculating the division of one integer, called the dividend, by another integer called the divisor, to produce a result called the quotient.
   a. Thing
   b. Long division0
   c. Undefined
   d. Undefined

142. In group theory, a _____ or monogenous group is a group that can be generated by a single element, in the sense that the group has an element g called a "generator" of the group such that, when written multiplicatively, every element of the group is a power of g a multiple of g when the notation is additive.
   a. Cyclic group0
   b. Thing
   c. Undefined
   d. Undefined

143. _____ has many meanings, most of which simply .
   a. Power0
   b. Thing
   c. Undefined
   d. Undefined

144. The _____ of two integers is the smallest positive integer that is a multiple of both intergers.
   a. Least common multiple0
   b. Thing
   c. Undefined
   d. Undefined

145. In mathematics, the _____ gives sufficient conditions for a polynomial to be irreducible over the rational numbers.
   a. Eisenstein criterion0
   b. Thing
   c. Undefined
   d. Undefined

146. _____ traditionally refers to the statistical process of determining comparable scores on different forms of an exam
   a. Equating0
   b. Thing
   c. Undefined
   d. Undefined

147. _____ is a method of mathematical proof typically used to establish that a given statement is true of all natural numbers
   a. Mathematical induction0
   b. Thing
   c. Undefined
   d. Undefined

148. In mathematics and the mathematical sciences, a _____ is a fixed, but possibly unspecified, value. This is in contrast to a variable, which is not fixed.
   a. Constant0
   b. Thing
   c. Undefined
   d. Undefined

149. _____ is a natural number that has exactly two distinct natural number divisors, which are 1 and the _____ itself.

Chapter 4. RINGS AND FIELDS

a. Prime number0
b. Thing
c. Undefined
d. Undefined

150. In mathematics, an _____ is a morphism (or homomorphism) from a mathematical object to itself. So, for example, an _____ of a vector space V is a linear map f : V → V and an _____ of a group G is a group homomorphism f : G → G, etc. In general, we can talk about endomorphisms in any category. In the category of sets, endomorphisms are simply maps from a set S into itself.
   a. Endomorphism0
   b. Thing
   c. Undefined
   d. Undefined

151. The _____ functions is determined by the nesting of two or more functions to form a single new function.
   a. Composition of two0
   b. Thing
   c. Undefined
   d. Undefined

152. _____, a field in mathematics, is the study of how functions change when their inputs change. The primary object of study in _____ is the derivative.
   a. Thing
   b. Differential calculus0
   c. Undefined
   d. Undefined

153. In mathematics, _____ are a non-commutative extension of complex numbers. They were first described by the Irish mathematician Sir William Rowan Hamilton in 1843 and applied to mechanics in three-dimensional space. At first, _____ were regarded as pathological, because they disobeyed the commutative law ab = ba. Although they have been superseded in most applications by vectors, they still find uses in both theoretical and applied mathematics, in particular for calculations involving three-dimensional rotations, such as in 3D computer graphics.
   a. Quaternions0
   b. Thing
   c. Undefined
   d. Undefined

154. In physics and in _____ calculus, a spatial _____, or simply _____, is a concept characterized by a magnitude and a direction.
   a. Thing
   b. Vector0
   c. Undefined
   d. Undefined

155. Sir _____ was an Irish mathematician, physicist, and astronomer who made important contributions to the development of optics, dynamics, and algebra. His discovery of quaternions is perhaps his best known investigation.
   a. Person
   b. William Rowan Hamilton0
   c. Undefined
   d. Undefined

156. In geometry, two lines or planes if one falls on the other in such a way as to create congruent adjacent angles. The term may be used as a noun or adjective. Thus, referring to Figure 1, the line AB is the _____ to CD through the point B.
   a. Thing
   b. Perpendicular0
   c. Undefined
   d. Undefined

157. _____ is a binary operation on two vectors in a three-dimensional Euclidean space that results in another vector which is perpedicular to the two input vectors.

Chapter 4. RINGS AND FIELDS

a. Cross product0
b. Thing
c. Undefined
d. Undefined

158. In geometry, _____ angles are angles that have a common ray coming out of the vertex going between two other rays.
   a. Concept
   b. Adjacent0
   c. Undefined
   d. Undefined

159. Order theory is a branch of mathematics that studies various kinds of binary relations that capture the intuitive notion of a mathematical _____.
   a. Thing
   b. Ordering0
   c. Undefined
   d. Undefined

160. A _____ is the sum of the elements of a sequence.
   a. Thing
   b. Series0
   c. Undefined
   d. Undefined

161. _____ in one variable is an infinite series of the form
   a. Thing
   b. Power series0
   c. Undefined
   d. Undefined

162. In mathematics, a _____ is a particular kind of polynomial, having just one term.
   a. Thing
   b. Monomial0
   c. Undefined
   d. Undefined

163. Mathematical _____ are demonstrations that, assuming certain axioms, some statement is necessarily true.
   a. Thing
   b. Proofs0
   c. Undefined
   d. Undefined

Chapter 5. IDEALS AND FACTOR RINGS

1. In abstract algebra, a _____ is a structure-preserving map between two algebraic structures. The word _____ comes from the Greek language: homo meaning "same" and morphi meaning "shape".
   a. Thing
   b. Homomorphism0
   c. Undefined
   d. Undefined

2. In mathematics, a _____ is an algebraic structure in which addition and multiplication are defined and have properties listed below.
   a. Ring0
   b. Thing
   c. Undefined
   d. Undefined

3. In mathematics, a _____ is an expression that is constructed from one or more variables and constants, using only the operations of addition, subtraction, multiplication, and constant positive whole number exponents. is a _____. Note in particular that division by an expression containing a variable is not in general allowed in polynomials. [1]
   a. Polynomial0
   b. Thing
   c. Undefined
   d. Undefined

4. In mathematics, an _____ (Greek:isos "equal", and morphe "shape") is a bijective map f such that both f and its inverse f^{-1} are homomorphisms, i.e. *structure-preserving* mappings.
   a. Isomorphism0
   b. Thing
   c. Undefined
   d. Undefined

5. In mathematics, the _____ inverse of a number x, denoted 1/x or x^{-1}, is the number which, when multiplied by x, yields 1. The _____ inverse of x is also called the reciprocal of x.
   a. Multiplicative0
   b. Thing
   c. Undefined
   d. Undefined

6. In mathematics, the _____ inverse, or opposite, of a number n is the number that, when added to n, yields zero. The _____ inverse of n is denoted −n.
   a. Thing
   b. Additive0
   c. Undefined
   d. Undefined

7. In mathematics, a _____ is any one of several different types of functions, mappings, operations, or transformations.
   a. Thing
   b. Projection0
   c. Undefined
   d. Undefined

8. An _____ is an equality that remains true regardless of the values of any variables that appear within it, to distinguish it from an equality which is true under more particular conditions.
   a. Thing
   b. Identity0
   c. Undefined
   d. Undefined

9. In mathematics, a _____ is a statement that can be proved on the basis of explicitly stated or previously agreed assumptions.
   a. Theorem0
   b. Thing
   c. Undefined
   d. Undefined

Chapter 5. IDEALS AND FACTOR RINGS

10. In mathematics the _____ of a set which is equipped with the operation of addition is an element which, when added to any other element x in the set, yields x.
    a. Concept
    b. Additive identity0
    c. Undefined
    d. Undefined

11. In mathematics, a _____ is a demonstration that, assuming certain axioms, some statement is necessarily true.
    a. Thing
    b. Proof0
    c. Undefined
    d. Undefined

12. An _____ or member of a set is an object that when collected together make up the set.
    a. Thing
    b. Element0
    c. Undefined
    d. Undefined

13. In mathematics, the _____ , or members of a set or more generally a class are all those objects which when collected together make up the set or class.
    a. Thing
    b. Elements0
    c. Undefined
    d. Undefined

14. In group theory, given a group G under a binary operation *, we say that some subset H of G is a _____ of G if H also forms a group under the operation *.
    a. Subgroup0
    b. Thing
    c. Undefined
    d. Undefined

15. In mathematics, an _____ (or neutral element) is a special type of element of a set with respect to a binary operation on that set.
    a. Concept
    b. Identity element0
    c. Undefined
    d. Undefined

16. A _____ is a mathematical statement which follows easily from a previously proven statement, typically a mathematical theorem.
    a. Corollary0
    b. Thing
    c. Undefined
    d. Undefined

17. In category theory and its applications to other branches of mathematics, _____ are a generalization of the kernels of group homomorphisms and the kernels of module homomorphisms and certain other kernels from algebra.
    a. Thing
    b. Kernel0
    c. Undefined
    d. Undefined

18. A _____ is a negotiable instrument instructing a financial institution to pay a specific amount of a specific currency from a specific demand account held in the maker/depositor's name with that institution. Both the maker and payee may be natural persons or legal entities.
    a. Thing
    b. Check0
    c. Undefined
    d. Undefined

19. In set theory and its applications throughout mathematics, _____ are a collection of sets (or sometimes other mathematical objects) that can be unambiguously defined by a property that all its members share.

Chapter 5. IDEALS AND FACTOR RINGS

a. Thing
b. Classes0
c. Undefined
d. Undefined

20. In mathematics, _____ is an elementary arithmetic operation. When one of the numbers is a whole number, _____ is the repeated sum of the other number.
    a. Multiplication0
    b. Thing
    c. Undefined
    d. Undefined

21. In mathematics, if G is a group, H a subgroup of G, and g an element of G, then, gH = {gh : h an element of H } is a left _____ of H in G, and Hg = {hg : h an element of H } is a right _____ of H in G.
    a. Thing
    b. Coset0
    c. Undefined
    d. Undefined

22. The _____, the average in everyday English, which is also called the arithmetic _____ (and is distinguished from the geometric _____ or harmonic _____). The average is also called the sample _____. The expected value of a random variable, which is also called the population _____.
    a. Thing
    b. Mean0
    c. Undefined
    d. Undefined

23. In mathematics, a _____ is the result of multiplying, or an expression that identifies factors to be multiplied.
    a. Product0
    b. Thing
    c. Undefined
    d. Undefined

24. In mathematics and the mathematical sciences, a _____ is a fixed, but possibly unspecified, value. This is in contrast to a variable, which is not fixed.
    a. Constant0
    b. Thing
    c. Undefined
    d. Undefined

25. _____ is a function whose values do not vary and thus are constant.
    a. Thing
    b. Constant function0
    c. Undefined
    d. Undefined

26. The mathematical concept of a _____ expresses the intuitive idea of deterministic dependence between two quantities, one of which is viewed as primary and the other as secondary. A _____ then is a way to associate a unique output for each input of a specified type, for example, a real number or an element of a given set.
    a. Thing
    b. Function0
    c. Undefined
    d. Undefined

27. In mathematics, a _____ number (or a _____) is a natural number that has exactly two (distinct) natural number divisors, which are 1 and the _____ number itself.
    a. Thing
    b. Prime0
    c. Undefined
    d. Undefined

28. In mathematics, a _____ of an integer n, also called a factor of n, is an integer which evenly divides n without leaving a remainder.

Chapter 5. IDEALS AND FACTOR RINGS

a. Divisor0
b. Thing
c. Undefined
d. Undefined

29. The _____ of a positive integer are the prime numbers that divide into that integer exactly, without leaving a remainder. The process of finding these numbers is called integer factorization, or prime factorization.
a. Thing
b. Prime factor0
c. Undefined
d. Undefined

30. In mathematics, _____ is the decomposition of an object into a product of other objects, or factors, which when multiplied together give the original.
a. Factoring0
b. Thing
c. Undefined
d. Undefined

31. In mathematics, factorization (British English: factorisation) or factoring is the decomposition of an object (for example, a number, a polynomial, or a matrix) into a product of other objects, or _____, which when multiplied together give the original.
a. Factors0
b. Thing
c. Undefined
d. Undefined

32. As an abstract term, _____ means similarity between objects.
a. Congruence0
b. Thing
c. Undefined
d. Undefined

33. In geometry, two sets are called _____ if one can be transformed into the other by an isometry, i.e., a combination of translations, rotations and reflections.
a. Congruent0
b. Thing
c. Undefined
d. Undefined

34. The _____ are the only integral domain whose positive elements are well-ordered, and in which order is preserved by addition. Like the natural numbers, the _____ form a countably infinite set. The set of all _____ is usually denoted in mathematics by a boldface Z .
a. Integers0
b. Thing
c. Undefined
d. Undefined

35. A _____ is a subset of a ring which shares many important properties of a prime number in the ring of integers.
a. Thing
b. Prime ideal0
c. Undefined
d. Undefined

36. Julius Wilhelm Richard _____ (October 6, 1831 – February 12, 1916) was a German mathematician who did important work in abstract algebra, algebraic number theory and the foundations of the real numbers.
a. Person
b. Dedekind0
c. Undefined
d. Undefined

37. In mathematics, an _____ is a complex number that is an algebraic element over the rational numbers.

Chapter 5. IDEALS AND FACTOR RINGS

a. Thing
b. Algebraic number0
c. Undefined
d. Undefined

38. The _____ is a measurement of how a function changes when the values of its inputs change.
a. Derivative0
b. Thing
c. Undefined
d. Undefined

39. A _____ is a construction in ring theory.
a. Quotient ring0
b. Thing
c. Undefined
d. Undefined

40. The _____ of a function is an extension of the concept of a sum, and are identified or found through the use of integration.
a. Integral0
b. Thing
c. Undefined
d. Undefined

41. In abstract algebra, a branch of mathematics, an _____ is a commutative ring with an additive identity 0 and a multiplicative identity 1 such that $0 \neq 1$, in which the product of any two non-zero elements is always non-zero.
a. Integral domain0
b. Thing
c. Undefined
d. Undefined

42. In mathematics, a _____ of a k-place relation $L \subseteq X_1 \times \ldots \times X_k$ is one of the sets X_j, $1 \leq j \leq k$. In the special case where k = 2 and $L \subseteq X_1 \times X_2$ is a function $L : X_1 \to X_2$, it is conventional to refer to X_1 as the _____ of the function and to refer to X_2 as the codomain of the function.
a. Domain0
b. Thing
c. Undefined
d. Undefined

43. In mathematics, a _____ is the end result of a division problem. It can also be expressed as the number of times the divisor divides into the dividend.
a. Quotient0
b. Thing
c. Undefined
d. Undefined

44. In mathematics, a _____ is a rectangular table of numbers or, more generally, a table consisting of abstract quantities that can be added and multiplied.
a. Thing
b. Matrix0
c. Undefined
d. Undefined

45. A _____, is a symbolized depiction of space which highlights relations between components of that space. Most usually a _____ is a two-dimensional, geometrically accurate representation of a three-dimensional space.
a. Thing
b. Map0
c. Undefined
d. Undefined

46. A _____ number is a positive integer which has a positive divisor other than one or itself.
a. Thing
b. Composite0
c. Undefined
d. Undefined

Chapter 5. IDEALS AND FACTOR RINGS

47. A _____, formed by the composition of one function on another, represents the application of the former to the result of the application of the latter to the argument of the composite.
   a. Thing
   b. Composite function0
   c. Undefined
   d. Undefined

48. A _____ is a set whose members are members of another set or a set contained within another set.
   a. Thing
   b. Subset0
   c. Undefined
   d. Undefined

49. A _____ is a ring in which the multiplication operation obeys the commutative law.
   a. Commutative ring0
   b. Thing
   c. Undefined
   d. Undefined

50. In mathematics, the _____ of two sets A and B is the set that contains all elements of A that also belong to B (or equivalently, all elements of B that also belong to A), but no other elements.
   a. Thing
   b. Intersection0
   c. Undefined
   d. Undefined

51. In mathematics, an _____ is a morphism (or homomorphism) from a mathematical object to itself. So, for example, an _____ of a vector space V is a linear map f : V → V and an _____ of a group G is a group homomorphism f : G → G, etc. In general, we can talk about endomorphisms in any category. In the category of sets, endomorphisms are simply maps from a set S into itself.
   a. Thing
   b. Endomorphism0
   c. Undefined
   d. Undefined

52. _____ is bother the congnitive process of transferring information from a particular subject , and a linguistic expression corresponding to such a process.
   a. Analogy0
   b. Thing
   c. Undefined
   d. Undefined

53. A _____ fraction is a fraction in which the absolute value of the numerator is less than the denominator--hence, the absolute value of the fraction is less than 1.
   a. Thing
   b. Proper0
   c. Undefined
   d. Undefined

54. In mathematics, a _____ is a group which is not the trivial group and whose only normal subgroups are the trivial group and the group itself.
   a. Thing
   b. Simple group0
   c. Undefined
   d. Undefined

55. In mathematics, an _____, also called a commutative group, is a group such that a * b= b*a for all and b in G. In other words, the order in which the binary operation is performed doesnt matter.
   a. Thing
   b. Abelian group0
   c. Undefined
   d. Undefined

Chapter 5. IDEALS AND FACTOR RINGS

56. In common philosophical language, a proposition or _____, is the content of an assertion, that is, it is true-or-false and defined by the meaning of a particular piece of language.
   a. Statement0
   b. Concept
   c. Undefined
   d. Undefined

57. _____ is a kind of property which exists as magnitude or multitude. It is among the basic classes of things along with quality, substance, change, and relation.
   a. Amount0
   b. Thing
   c. Undefined
   d. Undefined

58. The _____ of a ring R is defined to be the smallest positive integer n such that $n\,a = 0$, for all a in R.
   a. Characteristic0
   b. Thing
   c. Undefined
   d. Undefined

59. A _____ of a number is the product of that number with any integer.
   a. Thing
   b. Multiple0
   c. Undefined
   d. Undefined

60. _____ is a fixed, but possibly unspecified, value. This is in contrast to a variable, which is not fixed.
   a. Constant term0
   b. Thing
   c. Undefined
   d. Undefined

61. In mathematics, computing, linguistics, and related disciplines, an _____ is a finite list of well-defined instructions for accomplishing some task which, given an initial state, will terminate in a defined end-state.
   a. Algorithm0
   b. Concept
   c. Undefined
   d. Undefined

62. The _____ is a theorem in mathematics which precisely expresses the outcome of the usual process of division of integers. The name is something of a misnomer, as it is a theorem, not an algorithm, i.e. a well-defined procedure for achieving a specific task — although the _____ can be used to find the greatest common divisor of two integers.
   a. Thing
   b. Division Algorithm0
   c. Undefined
   d. Undefined

63. In group theory, a _____ or monogenous group is a group that can be generated by a single element, in the sense that the group has an element g called a "generator" of the group such that, when written multiplicatively, every element of the group is a power of g a multiple of g when the notation is additive.
   a. Cyclic group0
   b. Thing
   c. Undefined
   d. Undefined

64. In mathematics, there are several meanings of _____ depending on the subject.
   a. Thing
   b. Degree0
   c. Undefined
   d. Undefined

65. The _____ of measurement are a globally standardized and modernized form of the metric system.

a. Thing
b. Units0
c. Undefined
d. Undefined

66. In mathematics, a set is called _____ if there is a bijection between the set and some set of the form {1, 2, ..., n} where n is a natural number.
a. Thing
b. Finite0
c. Undefined
d. Undefined

67. A _____ is the result of the addition of a set of numbers. The numbers may be natural numbers, complex numbers, matrices, or still more complicated objects. An infinite _____ is a subtle procedure known as a series.
a. Sum0
b. Thing
c. Undefined
d. Undefined

68. In abstract algebra, a _____ is a non-zero ring that has no ideal besides the zero ideal and itself. A _____ can always be considered as a simple algebra.
a. Thing
b. Simple ring0
c. Undefined
d. Undefined

69. In mathematics, an _____ is essentially a set of common zeroes of a set of polynomials. They are one of the central objects of study in classical (and to some extent, modern) algebraic geometry.
a. Algebraic variety0
b. Thing
c. Undefined
d. Undefined

70. In mathematics, a _____ is a constant multiplicative factor of a certain object. The object can be such things as a variable, a vector, a function, etc. For example, the _____ of $9x^2$ is 9.
a. Coefficient0
b. Thing
c. Undefined
d. Undefined

71. _____ means of or relating to the French philosopher and mathematician René Descartes.
a. Thing
b. Cartesian0
c. Undefined
d. Undefined

72. In mathematics, the _____ is a direct product of sets. Specifically, the _____ of two sets X (for example the points on an x-axis) and Y (for example the points on a y-axis), denoted X × Y, is the set of all possible ordered pairs whose first component is a member of X and whose second component is a member of Y.
a. Thing
b. Cartesian product0
c. Undefined
d. Undefined

73. Compass and straightedge or ruler-and-compass _____ is the _____ of lengths or angles using only an idealized ruler and compass.
a. Construction0
b. Thing
c. Undefined
d. Undefined

74. The word _____ comes from the Latin word linearis, which means created by lines.

Chapter 5. IDEALS AND FACTOR RINGS

a. Thing
c. Undefined
b. Linear0
d. Undefined

75. _____ is a branch of mathematics concerning the study of structure, relation and quantity.
a. Algebra0
c. Undefined
b. Concept
d. Undefined

76. A _____ is a set of possible values that a variable can take on in order to satisfy a given set of conditions, which may include equations and inequalities.
a. Thing
c. Undefined
b. Solution set0
d. Undefined

77. In mathematics, _____ refers to the rewriting of an expression into a simpler form.
a. Reduction0
c. Undefined
b. Thing
d. Undefined

78. In mathematics, a matrix can be thought of as each row or _____ being a vector. Hence, a space formed by row vectors or _____ vectors are said to be a row space or a _____ space.
a. Column0
c. Undefined
b. Concept
d. Undefined

79. Order theory is a branch of mathematics that studies various kinds of binary relations that capture the intuitive notion of a mathematical _____.
a. Ordering0
c. Undefined
b. Thing
d. Undefined

80. _____ has many meanings, most of which simply .
a. Thing
c. Undefined
b. Power0
d. Undefined

81. In statistics, a _____ measure is one which is measuring what is supposed to measure.
a. Valid0
c. Undefined
b. Thing
d. Undefined

82. The _____ of two integers is the smallest positive integer that is a multiple of both intergers.
a. Least common multiple0
c. Undefined
b. Thing
d. Undefined

83. In mathematics, the notion of _____ is a generalization of the notion of invertible.
a. Cancellation0
c. Undefined
b. Thing
d. Undefined

84. A _____ is the part of the dividend that is left over when the dividend is not evenly divisible by the divisor.
a. Thing
c. Undefined
b. Remainder0
d. Undefined

Chapter 6. EXTENSION FIELDS

1. _____ is a set, with some particular properties and usually some additional structure, such as the operations of addition or multiplication, for instance.
   a. Thing
   b. Space0
   c. Undefined
   d. Undefined

2. In mathematics, a _____ is an expression that is constructed from one or more variables and constants, using only the operations of addition, subtraction, multiplication, and constant positive whole number exponents. is a _____. Note in particular that division by an expression containing a variable is not in general allowed in polynomials. [1]
   a. Polynomial0
   b. Thing
   c. Undefined
   d. Undefined

3. Compass and straightedge or ruler-and-compass _____ is the _____ of lengths or angles using only an idealized ruler and compass.
   a. Construction0
   b. Thing
   c. Undefined
   d. Undefined

4. A _____ is a simplified and structured visual representation of concepts, ideas, constructions, relations, statistical data, anatomy etc used in all aspects of human activities to visualize and clarify the topic.
   a. Diagram0
   b. Thing
   c. Undefined
   d. Undefined

5. In mathematics, a matrix can be thought of as each row or _____ being a vector. Hence, a space formed by row vectors or _____ vectors are said to be a row space or a _____ space.
   a. Column0
   b. Concept
   c. Undefined
   d. Undefined

6. In mathematics, a _____ is a statement that can be proved on the basis of explicitly stated or previously agreed assumptions.
   a. Thing
   b. Theorem0
   c. Undefined
   d. Undefined

7. An _____ or member of a set is an object that when collected together make up the set.
   a. Element0
   b. Thing
   c. Undefined
   d. Undefined

8. The _____ are the only integral domain whose positive elements are well-ordered, and in which order is preserved by addition. Like the natural numbers, the _____ form a countably infinite set. The set of all _____ is usually denoted in mathematics by a boldface Z .
   a. Thing
   b. Integers0
   c. Undefined
   d. Undefined

9. In mathematics, a _____ is a demonstration that, assuming certain axioms, some statement is necessarily true.
   a. Proof0
   b. Thing
   c. Undefined
   d. Undefined

10. In mathematics, if G is a group, H a subgroup of G, and g an element of G, then, gH = {gh : h an element of H } is a left _____ of H in G, and Hg = {hg : h an element of H } is a right _____ of H in G.

Chapter 6. EXTENSION FIELDS

a. Thing
b. Coset0
c. Undefined
d. Undefined

11. In mathematics, a _____ number is a real or complex number which is not algebraic, that is, not a solution of a non-zero polynomial equation, with rational coefficients.
    a. Thing
    b. Transcendental0
    c. Undefined
    d. Undefined

12. _____ is the logarithm to the base e, where e is an irrational constant approximately equal to 2.718281828459.
    a. Natural logarithm0
    b. Thing
    c. Undefined
    d. Undefined

13. In mathematics, a _____ may be described informally as a number that can be given by an infinite decimal representation.
    a. Real number0
    b. Thing
    c. Undefined
    d. Undefined

14. In mathematics, a _____ of a number x is the exponent y of the power by such that $x = b^y$. The value used for the base b must be neither 0 nor 1, nor a root of 1 in the case of the extension to complex numbers, and is typically 10, e, or 2.
    a. Logarithm0
    b. Thing
    c. Undefined
    d. Undefined

15. In mathematics, an _____ is a complex number that is an algebraic element over the rational numbers.
    a. Algebraic number0
    b. Thing
    c. Undefined
    d. Undefined

16. In mathematics, the _____ , or members of a set or more generally a class are all those objects which when collected together make up the set or class.
    a. Elements0
    b. Thing
    c. Undefined
    d. Undefined

17. In abstract algebra, a _____ is a structure-preserving map between two algebraic structures. The word _____ comes from the Greek language: homo meaning "same" and morphi meaning "shape".
    a. Thing
    b. Homomorphism0
    c. Undefined
    d. Undefined

18. In mathematics, there are several meanings of _____ depending on the subject.
    a. Degree0
    b. Thing
    c. Undefined
    d. Undefined

19. In mathematics and the mathematical sciences, a _____ is a fixed, but possibly unspecified, value. This is in contrast to a variable, which is not fixed.
    a. Thing
    b. Constant0
    c. Undefined
    d. Undefined

20. In category theory and its applications to other branches of mathematics, _____ are a generalization of the kernels of group homomorphisms and the kernels of module homomorphisms and certain other kernels from algebra.
   a. Kernel0
   b. Thing
   c. Undefined
   d. Undefined

21. In mathematics, _____ is the decomposition of an object into a product of other objects, or factors, which when multiplied together give the original.
   a. Thing
   b. Factoring0
   c. Undefined
   d. Undefined

22. In mathematics, a _____ is a constant multiplicative factor of a certain object. The object can be such things as a variable, a vector, a function, etc. For example, the _____ of $9x^2$ is 9.
   a. Coefficient0
   b. Thing
   c. Undefined
   d. Undefined

23. _____ has many meanings, most of which simply .
   a. Power0
   b. Thing
   c. Undefined
   d. Undefined

24. A _____ is a mathematical statement which follows easily from a previously proven statement, typically a mathematical theorem.
   a. Corollary0
   b. Thing
   c. Undefined
   d. Undefined

25. In mathematics, a _____ is the end result of a division problem. It can also be expressed as the number of times the divisor divides into the dividend.
   a. Quotient0
   b. Thing
   c. Undefined
   d. Undefined

26. In mathematics, a _____ number is a number which can be expressed as a ratio of two integers. Non-integer _____ numbers (commonly called fractions) are usually written as the vulgar fraction a / b, where b is not zero.
   a. Rational0
   b. Thing
   c. Undefined
   d. Undefined

27. In mathematics, a _____ is any function which can be written as the ratio of two polynomial functions.
   a. Rational function0
   b. Thing
   c. Undefined
   d. Undefined

28. The mathematical concept of a _____ expresses the intuitive idea of deterministic dependence between two quantities, one of which is viewed as primary and the other as secondary. A _____ then is a way to associate a unique output for each input of a specified type, for example, a real number or an element of a given set.
   a. Thing
   b. Function0
   c. Undefined
   d. Undefined

29. In mathematics, an _____ (Greek:isos "equal", and morphe "shape") is a bijective map f such that both f and its inverse f^{-1} are homomorphisms, i.e. *structure-preserving* mappings.

Chapter 6. EXTENSION FIELDS

a. Thing
b. Isomorphism0
c. Undefined
d. Undefined

30. In mathematics, _____ is an elementary arithmetic operation. When one of the numbers is a whole number, _____ is the repeated sum of the other number.
   a. Multiplication0
   b. Thing
   c. Undefined
   d. Undefined

31. In mathematics, a _____ is a number in the form of a + bi where a and b are real numbers, and i is the imaginary unit, with the property $i^2 = -1$. The real number a is called the real part of the _____, and the real number b is the imaginary part.
   a. Complex number0
   b. Thing
   c. Undefined
   d. Undefined

32. In mathematics, a _____ is the result of multiplying, or an expression that identifies factors to be multiplied.
   a. Product0
   b. Thing
   c. Undefined
   d. Undefined

33. In mathematics, factorization (British English: factorisation) or factoring is the decomposition of an object (for example, a number, a polynomial, or a matrix) into a product of other objects, or _____, which when multiplied together give the original.
   a. Factors0
   b. Thing
   c. Undefined
   d. Undefined

34. The word _____ comes from the Latin word linearis, which means created by lines.
   a. Linear0
   b. Thing
   c. Undefined
   d. Undefined

35. In arithmetic, _____ is a procedure for calculating the division of one integer, called the dividend, by another integer called the divisor, to produce a result called the quotient.
   a. Thing
   b. Long division0
   c. Undefined
   d. Undefined

36. A _____ fraction is a fraction in which the absolute value of the numerator is less than the denominator--hence, the absolute value of the fraction is less than 1.
   a. Proper0
   b. Thing
   c. Undefined
   d. Undefined

37. In plane geometry, a _____ is a polygon with four equal sides, four right angles, and parallel opposite sides. In algebra, the _____ of a number is that number multiplied by itself.
   a. Square0
   b. Thing
   c. Undefined
   d. Undefined

38. The _____ of a ring R is defined to be the smallest positive integer n such that $n a = 0$, for all a in R.

Chapter 6. EXTENSION FIELDS

a. Characteristic0
b. Thing
c. Undefined
d. Undefined

39. _____ is that branch of mathematics concerned with the study of groups. These are sets with a rule, or operation. The operation in a group must satisfy closure and have these three additional properties: 1) The operation must have the property of associativity. 2) There must be an identity element. 3) Every element must have a corresponding inverse element. _____ is used throughout mathematics and has several applications in physics and chemistry. Groups can be finite or infinite. A classification of finite simple groups, completed in 1983, is one of the major achievements of mathematics in the 20th century.

a. Group theory0
b. Thing
c. Undefined
d. Undefined

40. In mathematics, a _____ number (or a _____) is a natural number that has exactly two (distinct) natural number divisors, which are 1 and the _____ number itself.

a. Prime0
b. Thing
c. Undefined
d. Undefined

41. In mathematics, a set is called _____ if there is a bijection between the set and some set of the form {1, 2, ..., n} where n is a natural number.

a. Thing
b. Finite0
c. Undefined
d. Undefined

42. In physics and in _____ calculus, a spatial _____, or simply _____, is a concept characterized by a magnitude and a direction.

a. Thing
b. Vector0
c. Undefined
d. Undefined

43. _____ is a collection of objects called vectors that, informally speaking, may be scaled and added.

a. Vector space0
b. Thing
c. Undefined
d. Undefined

44. In linear algebra, real numbers are called scalars and relate to vectors in a vector space through the operation of _____ multiplication, in which a vector can be multiplied by a number to produce another vector.

a. Scalar0
b. Thing
c. Undefined
d. Undefined

45. _____ is a branch of mathematics concerning the study of structure, relation and quantity.

a. Concept
b. Algebra0
c. Undefined
d. Undefined

46. _____ is a mathematical subject that includes the study of limits, derivatives, integrals, and power series and constitutes a major part of modern university curriculum.

a. Thing
b. Calculus0
c. Undefined
d. Undefined

47. An _____ is any starting assumption from which other statements are logically derived

Chapter 6. EXTENSION FIELDS

a. Thing
b. Axiom0
c. Undefined
d. Undefined

48. A frame of _____ is a particular perspective from which the universe is observed.
    a. Thing
    b. Reference0
    c. Undefined
    d. Undefined

49. _____ was an Italian mathematician, whose work was of exceptional philosophical value. The author of over 200 books and papers, he was a founder of mathematical logic and set theory, to which he contributed much notation. The standard axiomatization of the natural numbers is named in his honor. He spent most of his career teaching mathematics at the University of Turin.
    a. Person
    b. Giuseppe Peano0
    c. Undefined
    d. Undefined

50. A _____ is a deliberate process for transforming one or more inputs into one or more results.
    a. Calculation0
    b. Thing
    c. Undefined
    d. Undefined

51. _____ was a German mathematician. Although much of his working life was spent in Zürich and then Princeton, he is closely identified with the University of Göttingen tradition of mathematics, represented by David Hilbert and Hermann Minkowski. His research has had major significance for theoretical physics as well as pure disciplines including number theory. He was one of the most influential mathematicians of the twentieth century, and a key member of the Institute for Advanced Study in its early years, in terms of creating an integrated and international view.
    a. Person
    b. Hermann Weyl0
    c. Undefined
    d. Undefined

52. _____ is one of the basic operations defining a vector space in linear algebra.
    a. Thing
    b. Scalar multiplication0
    c. Undefined
    d. Undefined

53. In mathematics, a _____ is an algebraic structure in which addition and multiplication are defined and have properties listed below.
    a. Ring0
    b. Thing
    c. Undefined
    d. Undefined

54. A _____ is a set whose members are members of another set or a set contained within another set.
    a. Subset0
    b. Thing
    c. Undefined
    d. Undefined

55. In mathematics, a _____ is a particular kind of polynomial, having just one term.
    a. Thing
    b. Monomial0
    c. Undefined
    d. Undefined

56. In combinatorial mathematics, a _____ is an un-ordered collection of unique elements.

Chapter 6. EXTENSION FIELDS

    a. Combination0
    c. Undefined
    b. Concept
    d. Undefined

57. In mathematics, a _____ occurs if there is a bijection between the set and some set of the form 1, 2, ..., n where n is a natural number.
    a. Finite set0
    c. Undefined
    b. Concept
    d. Undefined

58. An _____ is a combination of numbers, operators, grouping symbols and/or free variables and bound variables arranged in a meaningful way which can be evaluated..
    a. Thing
    c. Undefined
    b. Expression0
    d. Undefined

59. Mathematical _____ are demonstrations that, assuming certain axioms, some statement is necessarily true.
    a. Thing
    c. Undefined
    b. Proofs0
    d. Undefined

60. A _____ is 360° or 2∂ radians.
    a. Thing
    c. Undefined
    b. Turn0
    d. Undefined

61. In linear algebra and related areas of mathematics, the null vector or _____ is the vector in Euclidean space, all of whose components are zero.
    a. Zero vector0
    c. Undefined
    b. Thing
    d. Undefined

62. In mathematics, the _____ of two sets A and B is the set that contains all elements of A that also belong to B (or equivalently, all elements of B that also belong to A), but no other elements.
    a. Intersection0
    c. Undefined
    b. Thing
    d. Undefined

63. _____ is the property of two events happening at the same time in at least one reference frame.
    a. Simultaneous0
    c. Undefined
    b. Thing
    d. Undefined

64. In mathematics, an _____ is a theorem with a statement beginning 'there exist ...'. That is, in more formal terms of symbolic logic, it is a theorem with a statement involving the existential quantifier.
    a. Existence theorem0
    c. Undefined
    b. Thing
    d. Undefined

65. A _____ is an equation in which each term is either a constant or the product of a constant times the first power of a variable.
    a. Linear equation0
    c. Undefined
    b. Thing
    d. Undefined

Chapter 6. EXTENSION FIELDS

66. In mathematics, a _____ in elementary terms is any of a variety of different functions from geometry, such as rotations, reflections and translations.
   a. Transformation0
   b. Thing
   c. Undefined
   d. Undefined

67. In mathematics, a linear map also called a _____ or linear operator is a function between two vector spaces that preserves the operations of vector addition and scalar multiplication.
   a. Thing
   b. Linear transformation0
   c. Undefined
   d. Undefined

68. The _____, the average in everyday English, which is also called the arithmetic _____ (and is distinguished from the geometric _____ or harmonic _____). The average is also called the sample _____. The expected value of a random variable, which is also called the population _____.
   a. Mean0
   b. Thing
   c. Undefined
   d. Undefined

69. In number theory, the _____ of arithmetic (or unique factorization theorem) states that every natural number greater than 1 can be written as a unique product of prime numbers.
   a. Fundamental theorem0
   b. Concept
   c. Undefined
   d. Undefined

70. _____ states that every non-zero single-variable polynomial, with complex coefficients, has exactly as many complex roots as its degree, if repeated roots are counted up to their multiplicity.
   a. Thing
   b. Fundamental theorem of algebra0
   c. Undefined
   d. Undefined

71. In structural proof theory, an _____ is a proof whose structure is simple in a special way.
   a. Thing
   b. Analytic proof0
   c. Undefined
   d. Undefined

72. _____ is the state of being greater than any finite real or natural number, however large.
   a. Thing
   b. Infinite0
   c. Undefined
   d. Undefined

73. In mathematics, especially in order theory, an _____ of a subset S of some partially ordered set is an element of P which is greater than or equal to every element of S.
   a. Upper bound0
   b. Thing
   c. Undefined
   d. Undefined

74. _____ are groups whose members are members of another set or a set contained within another set.
   a. Subsets0
   b. Thing
   c. Undefined
   d. Undefined

75. In common philosophical language, a proposition or _____, is the content of an assertion, that is, it is true-or-false and defined by the meaning of a particular piece of language.

84 *Chapter 6. EXTENSION FIELDS*

   a. Statement0
   b. Concept
   c. Undefined
   d. Undefined

76. Order theory is a branch of mathematics that studies various kinds of binary relations that capture the intuitive notion of a mathematical _____.
   a. Ordering0
   b. Thing
   c. Undefined
   d. Undefined

77. _____ consists either of a suggested explanation for a phenomenon or of a reasoned proposal suggesting a possible correlation between multiple phenomena.
   a. Hypotheses0
   b. Event
   c. Undefined
   d. Undefined

78. Equivalence is the condition of being _____ or essentially equal.
   a. Equivalent0
   b. Thing
   c. Undefined
   d. Undefined

79. The _____ of a solid object is the three-dimensional concept of how much space it occupies, often quantified numerically.
   a. Volume0
   b. Thing
   c. Undefined
   d. Undefined

80. _____ is the collective allonym under which a group of (mainly French) 20th-century mathematicians wrote a series of books presenting an exposition of modern advanced mathematics, beginning in 1935. With the goal of founding all of mathematics on set theory, the group strove for utmost rigour and generality, creating some new terminology and concepts along the way.
   a. Nicolas Bourbaki0
   b. Thing
   c. Undefined
   d. Undefined

81. A _____ is the result of the addition of a set of numbers. The numbers may be natural numbers, complex numbers, matrices, or still more complicated objects. An infinite _____ is a subtle procedure known as a series.
   a. Thing
   b. Sum0
   c. Undefined
   d. Undefined

82. In mathematics, more specifically in abstract algebra, a _____ is the main object of study in field theory. The general idea is to start with a base field and construct in some manner a larger field which contains the base field and satisfies additional properties.
   a. Thing
   b. Field extension0
   c. Undefined
   d. Undefined

83. In mathematics, a _____ of a number x is a number r such that $r^2 = x$, or in words, a number r whose square (the result of multiplying the number by itself) is x.
   a. Thing
   b. Square root0
   c. Undefined
   d. Undefined

Chapter 6. EXTENSION FIELDS

84. The _____ of a function is an extension of the concept of a sum, and are identified or found through the use of integration.
    a. Integral0
    b. Thing
    c. Undefined
    d. Undefined

85. In abstract algebra, a branch of mathematics, an _____ is a commutative ring with an additive identity 0 and a multiplicative identity 1 such that 0 ≠ 1, in which the product of any two non-zero elements is always non-zero.
    a. Integral domain0
    b. Thing
    c. Undefined
    d. Undefined

86. In mathematics, a _____ of a complex-valued function f is a member x of the domain of f such that f(x) vanishes at x, that is, x : f (x) = 0.
    a. Thing
    b. Root0
    c. Undefined
    d. Undefined

87. In mathematics, a _____ of a k-place relation L ⊆ X_1 × ... × X_k is one of the sets X_j, 1 ≤ j ≤ k. In the special case where k = 2 and L ⊆ X_1 × X_2 is a function L : X_1 → X_2, it is conventional to refer to X_1 as the _____ of the function and to refer to X_2 as the codomain of the function.
    a. Thing
    b. Domain0
    c. Undefined
    d. Undefined

88. In mathematics, a _____ of an integer n, also called a factor of n, is an integer which evenly divides n without leaving a remainder.
    a. Thing
    b. Divisor0
    c. Undefined
    d. Undefined

89. In geometry, a line _____ is a part of a line that is bounded by two end points, and contains every point on the line between its end points.
    a. Segment0
    b. Concept
    c. Undefined
    d. Undefined

90. A _____ is a tool similar to a ruler, but without markings.
    a. Straightedge0
    b. Thing
    c. Undefined
    d. Undefined

91. A _____ is a part of a line that is bounded by two end points, and contains every point on the line between its end points.
    a. Line segment0
    b. Thing
    c. Undefined
    d. Undefined

92. In Euclidean geometry, a _____ is the set of all points in a plane at a fixed distance, called the radius, from a given point, the center.
    a. Thing
    b. Circle0
    c. Undefined
    d. Undefined

Chapter 6. EXTENSION FIELDS

93. In classical geometry, a _____ of a circle or sphere is any line segment from its center to its boundary. By extension, the _____ of a circle or sphere is the length of any such segment. The _____ is half the diameter. In science and engineering the term _____ of curvature is commonly used as a synonym for _____.
   a. Thing
   b. Radius0
   c. Undefined
   d. Undefined

94. A _____ is one of the basic shapes of geometry: a polygon with three vertices and three sides which are straight line segments.
   a. Triangle0
   b. Thing
   c. Undefined
   d. Undefined

95. In geometry, _____ lines are two lines that share one or more common points.
   a. Thing
   b. Intersecting0
   c. Undefined
   d. Undefined

96. In mathematics, a _____ is a number which can be expressed as a ratio of two integers. Non-integer rational numbers (commonly called fractions) are usually written as the vulgar fraction a / b, where b is not zero.
   a. Concept
   b. Rational Number0
   c. Undefined
   d. Undefined

97. A _____ is a set of numbers that designate location in a given reference system, such as x,y in a planar _____ system or an x,y,z in a three-dimensional _____ system.
   a. Coordinate0
   b. Thing
   c. Undefined
   d. Undefined

98. In mathematics, a _____ is a two-dimensional manifold or surface that is perfectly flat.
   a. Plane0
   b. Thing
   c. Undefined
   d. Undefined

99. In geometry, the _____ of an object is a point in some sense in the middle of the object.
   a. Center0
   b. Thing
   c. Undefined
   d. Undefined

100. In mathematics, science including computer science, linguistics and engineering, an _____ is, generally speaking, an independent variable or input to a function.
   a. Argument0
   b. Thing
   c. Undefined
   d. Undefined

101. In geometry, a _____ (Greek words diairo = divide and metro = measure) of a circle is any straight line segment that passes through the centre and whose endpoints are on the circular boundary, or, in more modern usage, the length of such a line segment. When using the word in the more modern sense, one speaks of the _____ rather than a _____, because all diameters of a circle have the same length. This length is twice the radius. The _____ of a circle is also the longest chord that the circle has.
   a. Thing
   b. Diameter0
   c. Undefined
   d. Undefined

Chapter 6. EXTENSION FIELDS

102. _____ is the middle point of a line segment.
  a. Thing
  b. Midpoint0
  c. Undefined
  d. Undefined

103. In geometry, two lines or planes if one falls on the other in such a way as to create congruent adjacent angles. The term may be used as a noun or adjective. Thus, referring to Figure 1, the line AB is the _____ to CD through the point B.
  a. Perpendicular0
  b. Thing
  c. Undefined
  d. Undefined

104. A _____ is a three-dimensional solid object bounded by six square faces, facets, or sides, with three meeting at each vertex.
  a. Cube0
  b. Thing
  c. Undefined
  d. Undefined

105. Leonhard _____ was a pioneering Swiss mathematician and physicist, who spent most of his life in Russia and Germany.
  a. Euler0
  b. Person
  c. Undefined
  d. Undefined

106. An _____ is an equality that remains true regardless of the values of any variables that appear within it, to distinguish it from an equality which is true under more particular conditions.
  a. Thing
  b. Identity0
  c. Undefined
  d. Undefined

107. In mathematics, a _____ section is a curve that can be formed by intersecting a cone with a plane.
  a. Conic0
  b. Thing
  c. Undefined
  d. Undefined

108. In geometry, a _____ is a special kind of point, usually a corner of a polygon, polyhedron, or higher dimensional polytope. In the geometry of curves a _____ is a point of where the first derivative of curvature is zero. In graph theory, a _____ is the fundamental unit out of which graphs are formed
  a. Thing
  b. Vertex0
  c. Undefined
  d. Undefined

109. In mathematics, a _____ function in the sense of algebraic geometry is an everywhere-defined, polynomial function on an algebraic variety V with values in the field K over which V is defined.
  a. Regular0
  b. Thing
  c. Undefined
  d. Undefined

110. Johann Carl Friedrich Gauss or _____ was a German mathematician and scientist of profound genius who contributed significantly to many fields, including number theory, analysis, differential geometry, geodesy, magnetism, astronomy, and optics.
  a. Person
  b. Carl Gauss0
  c. Undefined
  d. Undefined

Chapter 6. EXTENSION FIELDS

111. _____ is the mathematical action of repeatedly adding or subtracting one, usually to find out how many objects there are or to set aside a desired number of objects.
   a. Thing
   b. Counting0
   c. Undefined
   d. Undefined

112. In geometry, a _____ is any five-sided polygon.
   a. Pentagon0
   b. Thing
   c. Undefined
   d. Undefined

113. In mathematics, the _____ inverse of a number x, denoted 1/x or x^{-1}, is the number which, when multiplied by x, yields 1. The _____ inverse of x is also called the reciprocal of x.
   a. Thing
   b. Multiplicative0
   c. Undefined
   d. Undefined

114. An _____ of a number a is a number b such that $b^n=a$.
   a. Thing
   b. Nth root0
   c. Undefined
   d. Undefined

115. In mathematics, the nth _____ are all the complex numbers which yield 1 when raised to a given power n. It can be shown that they are located on the unit circle of the complex plane and that in that plane they form the vertices of an n-sided regular polygon with one vertex on 1.
   a. Thing
   b. Roots of unity0
   c. Undefined
   d. Undefined

116. The _____ is a measurement of how a function changes when the values of its inputs change.
   a. Derivative0
   b. Thing
   c. Undefined
   d. Undefined

117. In mathematical logic, a Gödel numbering (or Gödel _____) is a function that assigns to each symbol and well-formed formula of some formal language a unique natural number called its Gödel number.
   a. Code0
   b. Thing
   c. Undefined
   d. Undefined

118. In group theory, a _____ or monogenous group is a group that can be generated by a single element, in the sense that the group has an element g called a "generator" of the group such that, when written multiplicatively, every element of the group is a power of g a multiple of g when the notation is additive.
   a. Cyclic group0
   b. Thing
   c. Undefined
   d. Undefined

119. As an abstract term, _____ means similarity between objects.
   a. Thing
   b. Congruence0
   c. Undefined
   d. Undefined

120. In geometry, two sets are called _____ if one can be transformed into the other by an isometry, i.e., a combination of translations, rotations and reflections.

a. Thing
b. Congruent0
c. Undefined
d. Undefined

Chapter 7. ADVANCED GROUP THEORY

1. _____ is that branch of mathematics concerned with the study of groups. These are sets with a rule, or operation. The operation in a group must satisfy closure and have these three additional properties: 1) The operation must have the property of associativity. 2) There must be an identity element. 3) Every element must have a corresponding inverse element. _____ is used throughout mathematics and has several applications in physics and chemistry. Groups can be finite or infinite. A classification of finite simple groups, completed in 1983, is one of the major achievements of mathematics in the 20th century.
   a. Group theory0
   b. Thing
   c. Undefined
   d. Undefined

2. In mathematics, a _____ is a statement that can be proved on the basis of explicitly stated or previously agreed assumptions.
   a. Thing
   b. Theorem0
   c. Undefined
   d. Undefined

3. A _____ in mathematics, is a group G is called free if there is a subset S of G such that ny element of G can be written in one and only one way as a product of finitely many elements of S and their inverses.
   a. Thing
   b. Free group0
   c. Undefined
   d. Undefined

4. In mathematics, an _____ (Greek:isos "equal", and morphe "shape") is a bijective map f such that both f and its inverse f^{-1} are homomorphisms, i.e. *structure-preserving* mappings.
   a. Isomorphism0
   b. Thing
   c. Undefined
   d. Undefined

5. In mathematics, an _____, also called a commutative group, is a group such that a * b= b*a for all and b in G. In other words, the order in which the binary operation is performed doesnt matter.
   a. Thing
   b. Abelian group0
   c. Undefined
   d. Undefined

6. In category theory and its applications to other branches of mathematics, _____ are a generalization of the kernels of group homomorphisms and the kernels of module homomorphisms and certain other kernels from algebra.
   a. Thing
   b. Kernel0
   c. Undefined
   d. Undefined

7. In abstract algebra, a _____ is a structure-preserving map between two algebraic structures. The word _____ comes from the Greek language: homo meaning "same" and morphi meaning "shape".
   a. Thing
   b. Homomorphism0
   c. Undefined
   d. Undefined

8. In mathematics, a _____ is a demonstration that, assuming certain axioms, some statement is necessarily true.
   a. Thing
   b. Proof0
   c. Undefined
   d. Undefined

9. In group theory, given a group G under a binary operation *, we say that some subset H of G is a _____ of G if H also forms a group under the operation *.

Chapter 7. ADVANCED GROUP THEORY

    a. Thing   b. Subgroup0
    c. Undefined   d. Undefined

10. In mathematics, if G is a group, H a subgroup of G, and g an element of G, then, gH = {gh : h an element of H } is a left _____ of H in G, and Hg = {hg : h an element of H} is a right _____ of H in G.
    a. Coset0   b. Thing
    c. Undefined   d. Undefined

11. An _____ or member of a set is an object that when collected together make up the set.
    a. Element0   b. Thing
    c. Undefined   d. Undefined

12. In mathematics, the _____ , or members of a set or more generally a class are all those objects which when collected together make up the set or class.
    a. Elements0   b. Thing
    c. Undefined   d. Undefined

13. An _____ is an equality that remains true regardless of the values of any variables that appear within it, to distinguish it from an equality which is true under more particular conditions.
    a. Identity0   b. Thing
    c. Undefined   d. Undefined

14. In mathematics, the _____ of two sets A and B is the set that contains all elements of A that also belong to B (or equivalently, all elements of B that also belong to A), but no other elements.
    a. Thing   b. Intersection0
    c. Undefined   d. Undefined

15. A _____ is a simplified and structured visual representation of concepts, ideas, constructions, relations, statistical data, anatomy etc used in all aspects of human activities to visualize and clarify the topic.
    a. Thing   b. Diagram0
    c. Undefined   d. Undefined

16. In mathematics, a _____ is an ordered list of objects. Like a set, it contains members, also called elements or terms, and the number of terms is called the length of the _____. Unlike a set, order matters, and the exact same elements can appear multiple times at different positions in the _____.
    a. Sequence0   b. Thing
    c. Undefined   d. Undefined

17. A _____ is the sum of the elements of a sequence.
    a. Thing   b. Series0
    c. Undefined   d. Undefined

18. In mathematics, a set is called _____ if there is a bijection between the set and some set of the form {1, 2, ..., n} where n is a natural number.

a. Thing
b. Finite0
c. Undefined
d. Undefined

19. In mathematics, an _____ is something that does not change under a set of transformations. The property of being an _____ is invariance.
   a. Invariant0
   b. Thing
   c. Undefined
   d. Undefined

20. _____ Logic is a concept in traditional logic referring to a "type of immediate inference in which from a given proposition another proposition is inferred which has as its subject the predicate of the original proposition and as its predicate the subject of the original proposition (the quality of the proposition being retained)."
   a. Concept
   b. Converse0
   c. Undefined
   d. Undefined

21. _____ is the fee paid on borrowed money.
   a. Interest0
   b. Thing
   c. Undefined
   d. Undefined

22. In common philosophical language, a proposition or _____, is the content of an assertion, that is, it is true-or-false and defined by the meaning of a particular piece of language.
   a. Concept
   b. Statement0
   c. Undefined
   d. Undefined

23. In mathematics, science including computer science, linguistics and engineering, an _____ is, generally speaking, an independent variable or input to a function.
   a. Argument0
   b. Thing
   c. Undefined
   d. Undefined

24. In mathematics, the _____ is a technical result on the lattice of subgroups of a group.
   a. Butterfly lemma0
   b. Thing
   c. Undefined
   d. Undefined

25. In mathematics, a matrix can be thought of as each row or _____ being a vector. Hence, a space formed by row vectors or _____ vectors are said to be a row space or a _____ space.
   a. Column0
   b. Concept
   c. Undefined
   d. Undefined

26. In mathematics, a _____ of a positive integer n is a way of writing n as a sum of positive integers.
   a. Composition0
   b. Thing
   c. Undefined
   d. Undefined

27. In abstract algebra, a _____ provides a way to break up an algebraic structure, such as a group or a module, into simple pieces. The need for considering _____ in the context of modules arises from the fact that many naturally occuring modules are not semisimple, hence cannot be decomposed into a direct sum of simple modules. A _____ of a module M is a finite increasing filtration of M by submodules such that the successive quotients are simple and serves as a replacement of the direct sum decomposition of M into its simple constituents.

Chapter 7. ADVANCED GROUP THEORY

    a. Thing
    b. Composition series0
    c. Undefined
    d. Undefined

28. In mathematics, _____ is the decomposition of an object into a product of other objects, or factors, which when multiplied together give the original.
    a. Factoring0
    b. Thing
    c. Undefined
    d. Undefined

29. In mathematics, factorization (British English: factorisation) or factoring is the decomposition of an object (for example, a number, a polynomial, or a matrix) into a product of other objects, or _____, which when multiplied together give the original.
    a. Thing
    b. Factors0
    c. Undefined
    d. Undefined

30. _____ is the rearrangement of objects or symbols into distinguishable sequences.
    a. Permutation0
    b. Thing
    c. Undefined
    d. Undefined

31. In mathematics, a _____ of a complex-valued function f is a member x of the domain of f such that f(x) vanishes at x, that is, x : f (x) = 0.
    a. Thing
    b. Root0
    c. Undefined
    d. Undefined

32. In mathematics, a _____ is an expression that is constructed from one or more variables and constants, using only the operations of addition, subtraction, multiplication, and constant positive whole number exponents. is a _____. Note in particular that division by an expression containing a variable is not in general allowed in polynomials. [1]
    a. Thing
    b. Polynomial0
    c. Undefined
    d. Undefined

33. Marie Ennemond _____ was a French mathematician, known both for his foundational work in group theory and for his influential Cours d'analyse. He was born in Lyon and educated at the École polytechnique. He was an engineer by profession; later in life he taught at the École polytechnique and the Collège de France; where he had a reputation for eccentric choices of notation.
    a. Thing
    b. Camille Jordan0
    c. Undefined
    d. Undefined

34. Évariste _____ was a French mathematician born in Bourg-la-Reine.
    a. Person
    b. Galois0
    c. Undefined
    d. Undefined

35. _____ over a given field is a polynomial with coefficients in that field.
    a. Thing
    b. Algebraic equation0
    c. Undefined
    d. Undefined

36. In mathematics, a _____ is a countable collection of open covers of a topological space that satisfies certain separation axioms.

Chapter 7. ADVANCED GROUP THEORY

a. Development0
b. Thing
c. Undefined
d. Undefined

37. In plane geometry, a _____ is a polygon with four equal sides, four right angles, and parallel opposite sides. In algebra, the _____ of a number is that number multiplied by itself.
   a. Thing
   b. Square0
   c. Undefined
   d. Undefined

38. A _____ fraction is a fraction in which the absolute value of the numerator is less than the denominator--hence, the absolute value of the fraction is less than 1.
   a. Proper0
   b. Thing
   c. Undefined
   d. Undefined

39. _____ is the symbold used to indicate the nth root of a number
   a. Radical0
   b. Thing
   c. Undefined
   d. Undefined

40. In mathematics, _____ are used to indicate the square root of a number.
   a. Radicals0
   b. Thing
   c. Undefined
   d. Undefined

41. In geometry, the _____ of an object is a point in some sense in the middle of the object.
   a. Center0
   b. Thing
   c. Undefined
   d. Undefined

42. _____ is an adjective usually refering to being in the centre.
   a. Central0
   b. Thing
   c. Undefined
   d. Undefined

43. _____ is the state of being greater than any finite real or natural number, however large.
   a. Infinite0
   b. Thing
   c. Undefined
   d. Undefined

44. In mathematics, a _____ is the result of multiplying, or an expression that identifies factors to be multiplied.
   a. Thing
   b. Product0
   c. Undefined
   d. Undefined

45. In mathematics and logic, a _____ proof is a way of showing the truth or falsehood of a given statement by a straightforward combination of established facts, usually existing lemmas and theorems, without making any further assumptions.
   a. Thing
   b. Direct0
   c. Undefined
   d. Undefined

46. In mathematics, _____ is a part of the set theoretic notion of function.

Chapter 7. ADVANCED GROUP THEORY

a. Image0
b. Thing
c. Undefined
d. Undefined

47. In mathematics, specifically group theory, the _____, named after Ludwig Sylow, form a partial converse to Lagrange's theorem, which states that if H is a subgroup of a finite group G, then the order of H divides the order of G. The _____ guarantee, for certain divisors of the order of G, the existence of corresponding subgroups, and give information about the number of those subgroups.
a. Thing
b. Sylow theorems0
c. Undefined
d. Undefined

48. In number theory, the _____ of arithmetic (or unique factorization theorem) states that every natural number greater than 1 can be written as a unique product of prime numbers.
a. Concept
b. Fundamental theorem0
c. Undefined
d. Undefined

49. In abstract algebra, a _____ G is a subset S such that every element of G can be expressed as the product of finitely many elements of S and their inverses.
a. Thing
b. Generating set of a group0
c. Undefined
d. Undefined

50. In mathematics, a _____ number (or a _____) is a natural number that has exactly two (distinct) natural number divisors, which are 1 and the _____ number itself.
a. Thing
b. Prime0
c. Undefined
d. Undefined

51. _____ has many meanings, most of which simply .
a. Power0
b. Thing
c. Undefined
d. Undefined

52. In physics, an _____ is the path that an object makes around another object while under the influence of a source of centripetal force, such as gravity.
a. Thing
b. Orbit0
c. Undefined
d. Undefined

53. _____ is the mathematical action of repeatedly adding or subtracting one, usually to find out how many objects there are or to set aside a desired number of objects.
a. Thing
b. Counting0
c. Undefined
d. Undefined

54. In a mathematical proof or a syllogism, a _____ is a statement that is the logical consequence of preceding statements.
a. Concept
b. Conclusion0
c. Undefined
d. Undefined

55. Mathematical _____ are demonstrations that, assuming certain axioms, some statement is necessarily true.

Chapter 7. ADVANCED GROUP THEORY

   a. Proofs0
   c. Undefined
   b. Thing
   d. Undefined

56. In mathematics, a _____ of an integer n, also called a factor of n, is an integer which evenly divides n without leaving a remainder.
   a. Divisor0
   c. Undefined
   b. Thing
   d. Undefined

57. A _____ is a set of numbers that designate location in a given reference system, such as x,y in a planar _____ system or an x,y,z in a three-dimensional _____ system.
   a. Coordinate0
   c. Undefined
   b. Thing
   d. Undefined

58. _____, a Norwegian mathematician, was born in Nedstrand, near Finnoy where his father acted as rector.
   a. Niels Henrik Abel0
   c. Undefined
   b. Person
   d. Undefined

59. In Euclidean geometry, a _____ is moving every point a constant distance in a specified direction.
   a. Concept
   c. Undefined
   b. Translation0
   d. Undefined

60. A _____ is a mathematical statement which follows easily from a previously proven statement, typically a mathematical theorem.
   a. Corollary0
   c. Undefined
   b. Thing
   d. Undefined

61. Compass and straightedge or ruler-and-compass _____ is the _____ of lengths or angles using only an idealized ruler and compass.
   a. Construction0
   c. Undefined
   b. Thing
   d. Undefined

62. In algebra, a _____ is a binomial formed by taking the opposite of the second term of a binomial.
   a. Conjugate0
   c. Undefined
   b. Thing
   d. Undefined

63. In geometry, two sets are called _____ if one can be transformed into the other by an isometry, i.e., a combination of translations, rotations and reflections.
   a. Thing
   c. Undefined
   b. Congruent0
   d. Undefined

64. A _____ is a negotiable instrument instructing a financial institution to pay a specific amount of a specific currency from a specific demand account held in the maker/depositor's name with that institution. Both the maker and payee may be natural persons or legal entities.
   a. Check0
   c. Undefined
   b. Thing
   d. Undefined

Chapter 7. ADVANCED GROUP THEORY

65. In mathematics, an _____ is an isomorphism from a mathematical objct of itself while preserving all of its structure.
    a. Automorphism0
    b. Thing
    c. Undefined
    d. Undefined

66. A _____, is a symbolized depiction of space which highlights relations between components of that space. Most usually a _____ is a two-dimensional, geometrically accurate representation of a three-dimensional space.
    a. Thing
    b. Map0
    c. Undefined
    d. Undefined

67. In mathematics, a _____ is a group which is not the trivial group and whose only normal subgroups are the trivial group and the group itself.
    a. Thing
    b. Simple group0
    c. Undefined
    d. Undefined

68. In set theory and its applications throughout mathematics, _____ are a collection of sets (or sometimes other mathematical objects) that can be unambiguously defined by a property that all its members share.
    a. Thing
    b. Classes0
    c. Undefined
    d. Undefined

69. A _____ consists either of a suggested explanation for a phenomenon or of a reasoned proposal suggesting a possible correlation between multiple phenomena.
    a. Thing
    b. Hypothesis0
    c. Undefined
    d. Undefined

70. _____ consists either of a suggested explanation for a phenomenon or of a reasoned proposal suggesting a possible correlation between multiple phenomena.
    a. Hypotheses0
    b. Event
    c. Undefined
    d. Undefined

71. In mathematics, a _____ is a mathematical statement which appears likely to be true, but has not been formally proven to be true under the rules of mathematical logic.
    a. Concept
    b. Conjecture0
    c. Undefined
    d. Undefined

72. The word _____ is used in a variety of ways in mathematics.
    a. Thing
    b. Index0
    c. Undefined
    d. Undefined

73. _____ means "constancy", i.e. if something retains a certain feature even after we change a way of looking at it, then it is symmetric.
    a. Thing
    b. Symmetry0
    c. Undefined
    d. Undefined

74. In abstract algebra, a _____ group is an abelian that has a "basis" in the sense that every element of the group can be written in one and only one way as a finite linear combination of elements of the basis, with integer coefficient.

Chapter 7. ADVANCED GROUP THEORY

a. Free abelian0
b. Thing
c. Undefined
d. Undefined

75. Generally, a _____ is a splitting of something into parts.
   a. Thing
   b. Partition0
   c. Undefined
   d. Undefined

76. In mathematics, a _____ is a constant multiplicative factor of a certain object. The object can be such things as a variable, a vector, a function, etc. For example, the _____ of $9x^2$ is 9.
   a. Coefficient0
   b. Thing
   c. Undefined
   d. Undefined

77. An _____ is a combination of numbers, operators, grouping symbols and/or free variables and bound variables arranged in a meaningful way which can be evaluated..
   a. Thing
   b. Expression0
   c. Undefined
   d. Undefined

78. A _____ is a numeral used to indicate a count. The most common use of the word today is to name the part of a fraction that tells the number or count of equal parts.
   a. Numerator0
   b. Thing
   c. Undefined
   d. Undefined

79. _____ refers to the reduction of the body of a formerly living organism into simpler forms of matter.
   a. Decomposing0
   b. Thing
   c. Undefined
   d. Undefined

80. A _____ is the part of a fraction that tells how many equal parts make up a whole, and which is used in the name of the fraction: "halves", "thirds", "fourths" or "quarters", "fifths" and so on.
   a. Concept
   b. Denominator0
   c. Undefined
   d. Undefined

81. In mathematics, computing, linguistics, and related disciplines, an _____ is a finite list of well-defined instructions for accomplishing some task which, given an initial state, will terminate in a defined end-state.
   a. Concept
   b. Algorithm0
   c. Undefined
   d. Undefined

82. The _____ is a theorem in mathematics which precisely expresses the outcome of the usual process of division of integers. The name is something of a misnomer, as it is a theorem, not an algorithm, i.e. a well-defined procedure for achieving a specific task — although the _____ can be used to find the greatest common divisor of two integers.
   a. Thing
   b. Division Algorithm0
   c. Undefined
   d. Undefined

83. In abstract algebra, the term _____ refers to a number of concepts related to elements of finite order in groups and to the failure of modules to be free.

Chapter 7. ADVANCED GROUP THEORY

a. Thing
b. Torsion0
c. Undefined
d. Undefined

84. In the theory of abelian groups, the _____ A_T of an abelian group A is the subgroup of A consisting of all elements that have finite order. An abelian group A is called a torsion group if every element of A has finite order and is called torsion-free if every element of A except the identity is of infinite order.
a. Torsion subgroup0
b. Thing
c. Undefined
d. Undefined

85. In mathematics, a _____ number is a number which can be expressed as a ratio of two integers. Non-integer _____ numbers (commonly called fractions) are usually written as the vulgar fraction a / b, where b is not zero.
a. Rational0
b. Thing
c. Undefined
d. Undefined

86. In group theory, a _____ or monogenous group is a group that can be generated by a single element, in the sense that the group has an element g called a "generator" of the group such that, when written multiplicatively, every element of the group is a power of g a multiple of g when the notation is additive.
a. Cyclic group0
b. Thing
c. Undefined
d. Undefined

87. The _____, the average in everyday English, which is also called the arithmetic _____ (and is distinguished from the geometric _____ or harmonic _____). The average is also called the sample _____. The expected value of a random variable, which is also called the population _____.
a. Mean0
b. Thing
c. Undefined
d. Undefined

88. In mathematics, _____ is an elementary arithmetic operation. When one of the numbers is a whole number, _____ is the repeated sum of the other number.
a. Thing
b. Multiplication0
c. Undefined
d. Undefined

89. In mathematics, the additive inverse, or _____ of a number n is the number that, when added to n, yields zero. The additive inverse of n is denoted −n. For example, 7 is −7, because 7 + (−7) = 0, and the additive inverse of −0.3 is 0.3, because −0.3 + 0.3 = 0.
a. Thing
b. Opposite0
c. Undefined
d. Undefined

90. In mathematics, the _____ of a number n is the number that, when added to n, yields zero. The _____ of n is denoted −n. For example, 7 is −7, because 7 + (−7) = 0, and the _____ of −0.3 is 0.3, because −0.3 + 0.3 = 0.
a. Additive inverse0
b. Thing
c. Undefined
d. Undefined

91. _____ is a mathematical operation, written a^n, involving two numbers, the base a and the exponent n.
a. Thing
b. Exponentiating0
c. Undefined
d. Undefined

Chapter 7. ADVANCED GROUP THEORY

92. _____ is a mathematical operation, written a^n, involving two numbers, the base a and the exponent n.
   a. Exponentiation0
   b. Thing
   c. Undefined
   d. Undefined

93. In mathematics, the _____ gives an indication of the extent to which a certain binary operation fails to be commutative. There are different definitions used in group theory and ring theory.
   a. Thing
   b. Commutator0
   c. Undefined
   d. Undefined

94. In mathematics, a _____ occurs if there is a bijection between the set and some set of the form 1, 2, ..., n where n is a natural number.
   a. Finite set0
   b. Concept
   c. Undefined
   d. Undefined

95. Mathematical _____ is used to represent ideas.
   a. Thing
   b. Notation0
   c. Undefined
   d. Undefined

96. In mathematics, the _____ of order 2n is the abstract group of which one representation is the symmetry group in 2D of a regular polygon with n sides
   a. Thing
   b. Dihedral group0
   c. Undefined
   d. Undefined

97. _____ is a property that a binary operation can have.
   a. Associative law0
   b. Thing
   c. Undefined
   d. Undefined

98. In mathematics, the _____ inverse of a number x, denoted 1/x or x^{-1}, is the number which, when multiplied by x, yields 1. The _____ inverse of x is also called the reciprocal of x.
   a. Multiplicative0
   b. Thing
   c. Undefined
   d. Undefined

99. In mathematics, _____ are a non-commutative extension of complex numbers. They were first described by the Irish mathematician Sir William Rowan Hamilton in 1843 and applied to mechanics in three-dimensional space. At first, _____ were regarded as pathological, because they disobeyed the commutative law ab = ba. Although they have been superseded in most applications by vectors, they still find uses in both theoretical and applied mathematics, in particular for calculations involving three-dimensional rotations, such as in 3D computer graphics.
   a. Quaternions0
   b. Thing
   c. Undefined
   d. Undefined

100. A _____ is the part of the dividend that is left over when the dividend is not evenly divisible by the divisor.
   a. Thing
   b. Remainder0
   c. Undefined
   d. Undefined

Chapter 8. GROUPS IN TOPOLOGY

1. A _____ function is a function for which, intuitively, small changes in the input result in small changes in the output.
   a. Continuous0
   b. Event
   c. Undefined
   d. Undefined

2. In mathematics _____ is a certain general procedure to associate a sequence of abelian groups or modules with a given mathematical object such as a topological space singular _____ or a group.
   a. Thing
   b. Homology0
   c. Undefined
   d. Undefined

3. _____ is a branch of mathematics concerning the study of structure, relation and quantity.
   a. Concept
   b. Algebra0
   c. Undefined
   d. Undefined

4. _____ is a branch of mathematics that is an extension of geometry. _____ begins wiht a consideration of the nature of space, investigating both its fine structure and its global structure. _____ builds on set theory, considering both sets of points and families of sets.
   a. Thing
   b. Topology0
   c. Undefined
   d. Undefined

5. The mathematical concept of a _____ expresses the intuitive idea of deterministic dependence between two quantities, one of which is viewed as primary and the other as secondary. A _____ then is a way to associate a unique output for each input of a specified type, for example, a real number or an element of a given set.
   a. Thing
   b. Function0
   c. Undefined
   d. Undefined

6. _____ is a set, with some particular properties and usually some additional structure, such as the operations of addition or multiplication, for instance.
   a. Thing
   b. Space0
   c. Undefined
   d. Undefined

7. _____ element of an element x with respect to a binary operation * with identity element e is an element y such that x * y = y * x = e. In particular,
   a. Inverse0
   b. Thing
   c. Undefined
   d. Undefined

8. The _____, the average in everyday English, which is also called the arithmetic _____ (and is distinguished from the geometric _____ or harmonic _____). The average is also called the sample _____. The expected value of a random variable, which is also called the population _____.
   a. Mean0
   b. Thing
   c. Undefined
   d. Undefined

9. In the mathematical field of topology a _____ or topological isomorphism is a special isomorphism between topological spaces which respects topological properties.
   a. Homeomorphism0
   b. Thing
   c. Undefined
   d. Undefined

Chapter 8. GROUPS IN TOPOLOGY

10. In mathematics, an _____ (Greek:isos "equal", and morphe "shape") is a bijective map f such that both f and its inverse f $^{-1}$ are homomorphisms, i.e. *structure-preserving* mappings.
    a. Thing
    b. Isomorphism0
    c. Undefined
    d. Undefined

11. In mathematics, specifically in algebraic topology, _____ is a general term for a sequence of abelian groups defined from a cochain complex. That is, _____ is defined as the abstract study of cochains, cocycles, and coboundaries.
    a. Cohomology0
    b. Thing
    c. Undefined
    d. Undefined

12. In topology, two continuous functions from one topological space to another are called homotopic if one can be "continuously deformed" into the other, such a deformation being called a _____ between the two functions. An outstanding use of _____ is the definition of _____ groups and cohomotopy groups, important invariants in algebraic topology.
    a. Thing
    b. Homotopy0
    c. Undefined
    d. Undefined

13. A _____ is one of the basic shapes of geometry: a polygon with three vertices and three sides which are straight line segments.
    a. Thing
    b. Triangle0
    c. Undefined
    d. Undefined

14. In mathematics, the additive inverse, or _____ of a number n is the number that, when added to n, yields zero. The additive inverse of n is denoted −n. For example, 7 is −7, because 7 + (−7) = 0, and the additive inverse of −0.3 is 0.3, because −0.3 + 0.3 = 0.
    a. Opposite0
    b. Thing
    c. Undefined
    d. Undefined

15. _____ is the rearrangement of objects or symbols into distinguishable sequences.
    a. Permutation0
    b. Thing
    c. Undefined
    d. Undefined

16. In mathematics, the _____ of a number n is the number that, when added to n, yields zero. The _____ of n is denoted −n. For example, 7 is −7, because 7 + (−7) = 0, and the _____ of −0.3 is 0.3, because −0.3 + 0.3 = 0.
    a. Thing
    b. Additive inverse0
    c. Undefined
    d. Undefined

17. In mathematics, a _____ is an ordered list of objects. Like a set, it contains members, also called elements or terms, and the number of terms is called the length of the _____. Unlike a set, order matters, and the exact same elements can appear multiple times at different positions in the _____.
    a. Sequence0
    b. Thing
    c. Undefined
    d. Undefined

Chapter 8. GROUPS IN TOPOLOGY

18. In geometry, a _____ is a special kind of point, usually a corner of a polygon, polyhedron, or higher dimensional polytope. In the geometry of curves a _____ is a point of where the first derivative of curvature is zero. In graph theory, a _____ is the fundamental unit out of which graphs are formed
   a. Thing
   b. Vertex0
   c. Undefined
   d. Undefined

19. In mathematics, _____ geometry was the traditional name for the geometry of three-dimensional Euclidean space — for practical purposes the kind of space we live in.
   a. Solid0
   b. Thing
   c. Undefined
   d. Undefined

20. A _____ (plural: tetrahedra) is a polyhedron composed of four triangular faces, three of which meet at each vertex.
   a. Tetrahedron0
   b. Thing
   c. Undefined
   d. Undefined

21. In mathematics, an _____ on a real vector space is a choice of which ordered bases are "positively" oriented, or right-handed, and which are "negatively" oriented, or left-handed.
   a. Thing
   b. Orientation0
   c. Undefined
   d. Undefined

22. In mathematics, a set is called _____ if there is a bijection between the set and some set of the form {1, 2, ..., n} where n is a natural number.
   a. Thing
   b. Finite0
   c. Undefined
   d. Undefined

23. An _____ or member of a set is an object that when collected together make up the set.
   a. Thing
   b. Element0
   c. Undefined
   d. Undefined

24. A _____ is the result of the addition of a set of numbers. The numbers may be natural numbers, complex numbers, matrices, or still more complicated objects. An infinite _____ is a subtle procedure known as a series.
   a. Thing
   b. Sum0
   c. Undefined
   d. Undefined

25. In mathematics, a _____ is a constant multiplicative factor of a certain object. The object can be such things as a variable, a vector, a function, etc. For example, the _____ of $9x^2$ is 9.
   a. Thing
   b. Coefficient0
   c. Undefined
   d. Undefined

26. In abstract algebra, a _____ group is an abelian that has a "basis" in the sense that every element of the group can be written in one and only one way as a finite linear combination of elements of the basis, with integer coefficient.
   a. Thing
   b. Free abelian0
   c. Undefined
   d. Undefined

27. In mathematics, an _____, also called a commutative group, is a group such that a * b= b*a for all and b in G. In other words, the order in which the binary operation is performed doesnt matter.

a. Thing
c. Undefined
b. Abelian group0
d. Undefined

28. In category theory and its applications to other branches of mathematics, _____ are a generalization of the kernels of group homomorphisms and the kernels of module homomorphisms and certain other kernels from algebra.
   a. Kernel0
   c. Undefined
   b. Thing
   d. Undefined

29. In abstract algebra, a _____ is a structure-preserving map between two algebraic structures. The word _____ comes from the Greek language: homo meaning "same" and morphi meaning "shape".
   a. Thing
   c. Undefined
   b. Homomorphism0
   d. Undefined

30. In mathematics, _____ is a part of the set theoretic notion of function.
   a. Thing
   c. Undefined
   b. Image0
   d. Undefined

31. _____ is the fee paid on borrowed money.
   a. Thing
   c. Undefined
   b. Interest0
   d. Undefined

32. In mathematics, the _____ , or members of a set or more generally a class are all those objects which when collected together make up the set or class.
   a. Elements0
   c. Undefined
   b. Thing
   d. Undefined

33. Mathematical _____ is used to represent ideas.
   a. Notation0
   c. Undefined
   b. Thing
   d. Undefined

34. An _____ is an equality that remains true regardless of the values of any variables that appear within it, to distinguish it from an equality which is true under more particular conditions.
   a. Thing
   c. Undefined
   b. Identity0
   d. Undefined

35. The _____ of a member of a multiset is how many memberships in the multiset it has.
   a. Thing
   c. Undefined
   b. Multiplicity0
   d. Undefined

36. _____ is the mathematical action of repeatedly adding or subtracting one, usually to find out how many objects there are or to set aside a desired number of objects.
   a. Thing
   c. Undefined
   b. Counting0
   d. Undefined

37. In topology, the _____ are subsets S of a topological space X is the set of points which can be approached both from S and from the outside of S.

Chapter 8. GROUPS IN TOPOLOGY

a. Boundaries0
b. Thing
c. Undefined
d. Undefined

38. In mathematics, science including computer science, linguistics and engineering, an _____ is, generally speaking, an independent variable or input to a function.
a. Thing
b. Argument0
c. Undefined
d. Undefined

39. A _____ of a number is the product of that number with any integer.
a. Multiple0
b. Thing
c. Undefined
d. Undefined

40. In mathematics, if G is a group, H a subgroup of G, and g an element of G, then, gH = {gh : h an element of H } is a left _____ of H in G, and Hg = {hg : h an element of H } is a right _____ of H in G.
a. Coset0
b. Thing
c. Undefined
d. Undefined

41. _____ is the state of being greater than any finite real or natural number, however large.
a. Thing
b. Infinite0
c. Undefined
d. Undefined

42. In mathematics, an inequality is a statement about the relative size or order of two objects. For example 14 > 10, or 14 is _____ 10.
a. Greater than0
b. Thing
c. Undefined
d. Undefined

43. In mathematics, a _____ is the set of all points in three-dimensional space (R^3) which are at distance r from a fixed point of that space, where r is a positive real number called the radius of the _____. The fixed point is called the center or centre, and is not part of the _____ itself.
a. Thing
b. Sphere0
c. Undefined
d. Undefined

44. In trigonometry and elementary geometry, _____ is the process of finding coordinates and distance to a point by calculating the length of one side of a triangle, given measurements of angles and sides of the triangle formed by that point and two other known reference points, using the law of sines.
a. Thing
b. Triangulation0
c. Undefined
d. Undefined

45. Around 300 BC, the Greek mathematician Euclid laid down the rules of what has now come to be called "Euclidean geometry", which is the study of the relationships between angles and distances in space. Euclid first developed "plane geometry" which dealt with the geometry of two-dimensional objects on a flat surface. He then went on to develop "solid geometry" which analyzed the geometry of three-dimensional objects. All of the axioms of Euclid have been encoded into an abstract mathematical space known as a two- or three-dimensional _____. These mathematical spaces may be extended to apply to any dimension, and such a space is called an n-dimensional _____.

a. Thing
b. Euclidean space0
c. Undefined
d. Undefined

46. In mathematics, a _____ is a demonstration that, assuming certain axioms, some statement is necessarily true.
   a. Proof0
   b. Thing
   c. Undefined
   d. Undefined

47. Mathematical _____ are demonstrations that, assuming certain axioms, some statement is necessarily true.
   a. Proofs0
   b. Thing
   c. Undefined
   d. Undefined

48. In Euclidean geometry, a _____ is the set of all points in a plane at a fixed distance, called the radius, from a given point, the center.
   a. Thing
   b. Circle0
   c. Undefined
   d. Undefined

49. In mathematics, the _____ of a coordinate system is the point where the axes of the system intersect.
   a. Thing
   b. Origin0
   c. Undefined
   d. Undefined

50. An _____ is a type of quadric surface that is a higher dimensional analogue of an ellipse.
   a. Ellipsoid0
   b. Thing
   c. Undefined
   d. Undefined

51. In classical geometry, a _____ of a circle or sphere is any line segment from its center to its boundary. By extension, the _____ of a circle or sphere is the length of any such segment. The _____ is half the diameter. In science and engineering the term _____ of curvature is commonly used as a synonym for _____.
   a. Radius0
   b. Thing
   c. Undefined
   d. Undefined

52. An _____ is a combination of numbers, operators, grouping symbols and/or free variables and bound variables arranged in a meaningful way which can be evaluated..
   a. Expression0
   b. Thing
   c. Undefined
   d. Undefined

53. In mathematics, factorization (British English: factorisation) or factoring is the decomposition of an object (for example, a number, a polynomial, or a matrix) into a product of other objects, or _____, which when multiplied together give the original.
   a. Thing
   b. Factors0
   c. Undefined
   d. Undefined

54. In mathematics, a _____ is a statement that can be proved on the basis of explicitly stated or previously agreed assumptions.
   a. Thing
   b. Theorem0
   c. Undefined
   d. Undefined

Chapter 8. GROUPS IN TOPOLOGY

55. In mathematics, in the field of group theory, a _____ of a group is a quasisimple subnormal subgroup.
    a. Component0
    b. Concept
    c. Undefined
    d. Undefined

56. In geometry, the _____ of an object is a point in some sense in the middle of the object.
    a. Thing
    b. Center0
    c. Undefined
    d. Undefined

57. In mathematics, a _____ is a connected curve that does not intersect itself and ends at the same point in which it starts.
    a. Thing
    b. Closed curve0
    c. Undefined
    d. Undefined

58. In mathematics, the concept of a _____ tries to capture the intuitive idea of a geometrical one-dimensional and continuous object. A simple example is the circle.
    a. Curve0
    b. Thing
    c. Undefined
    d. Undefined

59. In mathematics, _____ are the intuitive idea of a geometrical one-dimensional and continuous object.
    a. Thing
    b. Curves0
    c. Undefined
    d. Undefined

60. _____ is a kind of property which exists as magnitude or multitude. It is among the basic classes of things along with quality, substance, change, and relation.
    a. Thing
    b. Amount0
    c. Undefined
    d. Undefined

61. Deductive _____ is the kind of _____ in which the conclusion is necessitated by, or reached from, previously known facts (the premises).
    a. Reasoning0
    b. Thing
    c. Undefined
    d. Undefined

62. _____ is the study of terms and their use — of words and compound words that are used in specific contexts.
    a. Terminology0
    b. Thing
    c. Undefined
    d. Undefined

63. In geometry, a _____ is a surface of revolution generated by revolving a circle in three dimensional space about an axis coplanar with the circle, which does not touch the circle. Examples of tori include the surfaces of doughnuts and inner tubes. A circle rotated about a chord of the circle is called a _____ in some contexts, but this is not a common usage in mathematics. The shape produced when a circle is rotated about a chord resembles a round cushion. _____ was the Latin word for a cushion of this shape.
    a. Torus0
    b. Thing
    c. Undefined
    d. Undefined

Chapter 8. GROUPS IN TOPOLOGY

64. The _____ are the only integral domain whose positive elements are well-ordered, and in which order is preserved by addition. Like the natural numbers, the _____ form a countably infinite set. The set of all _____ is usually denoted in mathematics by a boldface Z .
   a. Thing
   b. Integers0
   c. Undefined
   d. Undefined

65. In geometry, _____ angles are angles that have a common ray coming out of the vertex going between two other rays.
   a. Concept
   b. Adjacent0
   c. Undefined
   d. Undefined

66. In trigonometry, the _____ is a function defined as $\tan x = \sin x / \cos x$. The function is so-named because it can be defined as the length of a certain segment of a _____ (in the geometric sense) to the unit circle. In plane geometry, a line is _____ to a curve, at some point, if both line and curve pass through the point with the same direction.
   a. Thing
   b. Tangent0
   c. Undefined
   d. Undefined

67. In mathematics, a _____ is an algebraic structure in which addition and multiplication are defined and have properties listed below.
   a. Thing
   b. Ring0
   c. Undefined
   d. Undefined

68. _____ is a circle on the surface of a sphere that has the same circumference as the sphere, dividing the sphere into two equal hemispheres.
   a. Thing
   b. Great circle0
   c. Undefined
   d. Undefined

69. In abstract algebra, the term _____ refers to a number of concepts related to elements of finite order in groups and to the failure of modules to be free.
   a. Thing
   b. Torsion0
   c. Undefined
   d. Undefined

70. In the theory of abelian groups, the _____ A_T of an abelian group A is the subgroup of A consisting of all elements that have finite order. An abelian group A is called a torsion group if every element of A has finite order and is called torsion-free if every element of A except the identity is of infinite order.
   a. Torsion subgroup0
   b. Thing
   c. Undefined
   d. Undefined

71. In group theory, given a group G under a binary operation *, we say that some subset H of G is a _____ of G if H also forms a group under the operation *.
   a. Subgroup0
   b. Thing
   c. Undefined
   d. Undefined

72. In geometry, a _____ is defined as a quadrilateral where all four of its angles are right angles.

Chapter 8. GROUPS IN TOPOLOGY

a. Thing
b. Rectangle0
c. Undefined
d. Undefined

73. In Euclidean geometry, an _____ is a closed segment of a differentiable curve in the two-dimensional plane; for example, a circular _____ is a segment of a circle.
a. Concept
b. Arc0
c. Undefined
d. Undefined

74. A _____, is a symbolized depiction of space which highlights relations between components of that space. Most usually a _____ is a two-dimensional, geometrically accurate representation of a three-dimensional space.
a. Thing
b. Map0
c. Undefined
d. Undefined

75. _____ is the distance around a given two-dimensional object. As a general rule, the _____ of a polygon can always be calculated by adding all the length of the sides together. So, the formula for triangles is P = a + b + c, where a, b and c stand for each side of it. For quadrilaterals the equation is P = a + b + c + d. For equilateral polygons, P = na, where n is the number of sides and a is the side length.
a. Thing
b. Perimeter0
c. Undefined
d. Undefined

76. In mathematics, the _____ f is the collection of all ordered pairs . In particular, graph means the graphical representation of this collection, in the form of a curve or surface, together with axes, etc. Graphing on a Cartesian plane is sometimes referred to as curve sketching.
a. Graph of a function0
b. Thing
c. Undefined
d. Undefined

77. In plane geometry, a _____ is a polygon with four equal sides, four right angles, and parallel opposite sides. In algebra, the _____ of a number is that number multiplied by itself.
a. Square0
b. Thing
c. Undefined
d. Undefined

78. A _____ can refer to a line joining two nonadjacent vertices of a polygon or polyhedron, or in some contexts any upward or downward sloping line. .
a. Diagonal0
b. Thing
c. Undefined
d. Undefined

79. In geometry, a line _____ is a part of a line that is bounded by two end points, and contains every point on the line between its end points.
a. Segment0
b. Concept
c. Undefined
d. Undefined

80. A _____ is a part of a line that is bounded by two end points, and contains every point on the line between its end points.
a. Line segment0
b. Thing
c. Undefined
d. Undefined

Chapter 8. GROUPS IN TOPOLOGY

81. A _____ fraction is a fraction in which the absolute value of the numerator is less than the denominator--hence, the absolute value of the fraction is less than 1.
   a. Thing
   b. Proper0
   c. Undefined
   d. Undefined

82. A _____ is a deliberate process for transforming one or more inputs into one or more results.
   a. Thing
   b. Calculation0
   c. Undefined
   d. Undefined

83. In mathematics and logic, a _____ proof is a way of showing the truth or falsehood of a given statement by a straightforward combination of established facts, usually existing lemmas and theorems, without making any further assumptions.
   a. Thing
   b. Direct0
   c. Undefined
   d. Undefined

84. The _____ of a ring R is defined to be the smallest positive integer n such that n a = 0, for all a in R.
   a. Characteristic0
   b. Thing
   c. Undefined
   d. Undefined

85. Leonhard _____ was a pioneering Swiss mathematician and physicist, who spent most of his life in Russia and Germany.
   a. Euler0
   b. Person
   c. Undefined
   d. Undefined

86. The _____ is a topological invariant, a number that describes one aspect of a topological space's shape or structure.
   a. Thing
   b. Euler characteristic0
   c. Undefined
   d. Undefined

87. In mathematics, a _____ is a two-dimensional manifold or surface that is perfectly flat.
   a. Thing
   b. Plane0
   c. Undefined
   d. Undefined

88. In physics, _____ is the rate of change of acceleration; more precisely, the derivative of acceleration with respect to time, the second derivative of velocity, or the third derivative of displacement. _____ is described by the following equation:
   a. Jerk0
   b. Thing
   c. Undefined
   d. Undefined

89. In mathematics, a _____ is a construct originally used in the field of algebraic topology. It is an algebraic means of representing the relationships between the cycles and boundaries in various dimensions of some "space".
   a. Thing
   b. Chain Complex0
   c. Undefined
   d. Undefined

90. A _____ is a number, figure, or indicator that appears below the normal line of type, typically used in a formula, mathematical expression, or description of a chemical compound.

Chapter 8. GROUPS IN TOPOLOGY

a. Thing
b. Subscript0
c. Undefined
d. Undefined

91. A _____ is a simplified and structured visual representation of concepts, ideas, constructions, relations, statistical data, anatomy etc used in all aspects of human activities to visualize and clarify the topic.
    a. Thing
    b. Diagram0
    c. Undefined
    d. Undefined

92. A _____ is a negotiable instrument instructing a financial institution to pay a specific amount of a specific currency from a specific demand account held in the maker/depositor's name with that institution. Both the maker and payee may be natural persons or legal entities.
    a. Check0
    b. Thing
    c. Undefined
    d. Undefined

93. _____ means in succession or back-to-back
    a. Consecutive0
    b. Thing
    c. Undefined
    d. Undefined

94. In mathematics, the _____ inverse, or opposite, of a number n is the number that, when added to n, yields zero. The _____ inverse of n is denoted −n.
    a. Thing
    b. Additive0
    c. Undefined
    d. Undefined

Chapter 9. FACTORIZATION

1. In mathematics, the _____ inverse of a number x, denoted 1/x or x^{-1}, is the number which, when multiplied by x, yields 1. The _____ inverse of x is also called the reciprocal of x.
   a. Multiplicative0
   b. Thing
   c. Undefined
   d. Undefined

2. A _____ is a commutative ring in which every element can be uniquely written as a product of prime elements, analogous to the fundamental theorem of arithmetic for the integers.
   a. Thing
   b. Unique factorization domain0
   c. Undefined
   d. Undefined

3. In mathematics, a _____ number (or a _____) is a natural number that has exactly two (distinct) natural number divisors, which are 1 and the _____ number itself.
   a. Thing
   b. Prime0
   c. Undefined
   d. Undefined

4. In abstract algebra, a _____ is a type of ring in which the Euclidean algorithm can be used. More precisely, a _____ is an integral domain D on which one can define a function v mapping nonzero elements of D to non-negative integers that satisfies the following division-with-remainder property: If a and b are in D and b is nonzero, then there are q and r in D such that a = bq + r and either r = 0 or v(r) < v(b).
   a. Thing
   b. Euclidean domain0
   c. Undefined
   d. Undefined

5. In mathematics, _____ is the decomposition of an object into a product of other objects, or factors, which when multiplied together give the original.
   a. Factoring0
   b. Thing
   c. Undefined
   d. Undefined

6. The _____ are the only integral domain whose positive elements are well-ordered, and in which order is preserved by addition. Like the natural numbers, the _____ form a countably infinite set. The set of all _____ is usually denoted in mathematics by a boldface Z .
   a. Integers0
   b. Thing
   c. Undefined
   d. Undefined

7. The _____ of a function is an extension of the concept of a sum, and are identified or found through the use of integration.
   a. Integral0
   b. Thing
   c. Undefined
   d. Undefined

8. In abstract algebra, a branch of mathematics, an _____ is a commutative ring with an additive identity 0 and a multiplicative identity 1 such that 0 ≠ 1, in which the product of any two non-zero elements is always non-zero.
   a. Integral domain0
   b. Thing
   c. Undefined
   d. Undefined

9. In mathematics, a _____ of a k-place relation $L \subseteq X_1 \times ... \times X_k$ is one of the sets X_j, $1 \le j \le k$. In the special case where k = 2 and $L \subseteq X_1 \times X_2$ is a function $L : X_1 \to X_2$, it is conventional to refer to X_1 as the _____ of the function and to refer to X_2 as the codomain of the function.

Chapter 9. FACTORIZATION

   a. Thing
   c. Undefined
   b. Domain0
   d. Undefined

10. A frame of _____ is a particular perspective from which the universe is observed.
   a. Thing
   c. Undefined
   b. Reference0
   d. Undefined

11. A _____ is a ring in which the multiplication operation obeys the commutative law.
   a. Thing
   c. Undefined
   b. Commutative ring0
   d. Undefined

12. In mathematics, a _____ is an algebraic structure in which addition and multiplication are defined and have properties listed below.
   a. Thing
   c. Undefined
   b. Ring0
   d. Undefined

13. In mathematics, the _____ of a number x, denoted 1/x or x^{-1}, is the number which, when multiplied by x, yields 1. The _____ of x is also called the reciprocal of x.
   a. Multiplicative inverse0
   c. Undefined
   b. Thing
   d. Undefined

14. The _____ of measurement are a globally standardized and modernized form of the metric system.
   a. Thing
   c. Undefined
   b. Units0
   d. Undefined

15. An _____ or member of a set is an object that when collected together make up the set.
   a. Element0
   c. Undefined
   b. Thing
   d. Undefined

16. In mathematics, the _____ , or members of a set or more generally a class are all those objects which when collected together make up the set or class.
   a. Thing
   c. Undefined
   b. Elements0
   d. Undefined

17. An _____ is a binary relation between two elements of a set which groups them together as being equivalent in some way.
   a. Equivalence relation0
   c. Undefined
   b. Thing
   d. Undefined

18. _____ element of an element x with respect to a binary operation * with identity element e is an element y such that x * y = y * x = e. In particular,
   a. Inverse0
   c. Undefined
   b. Thing
   d. Undefined

19. In mathematics, a _____ is a demonstration that, assuming certain axioms, some statement is necessarily true.

a. Proof0
b. Thing
c. Undefined
d. Undefined

20. In mathematics, a _____ is a statement that can be proved on the basis of explicitly stated or previously agreed assumptions.
   a. Theorem0
   b. Thing
   c. Undefined
   d. Undefined

21. In mathematics, a _____ is a mathematical statement which appears likely to be true, but has not been formally proven to be true under the rules of mathematical logic.
   a. Conjecture0
   b. Concept
   c. Undefined
   d. Undefined

22. In mathematics, a _____ of a complex-valued function f is a member x of the domain of f such that f(x) vanishes at x, that is, x : f (x) = 0.
   a. Root0
   b. Thing
   c. Undefined
   d. Undefined

23. In mathematics, a _____ is a number in the form of a + bi where a and b are real numbers, and i is the imaginary unit, with the property i 2 = −1. The real number a is called the real part of the _____, and the real number b is the imaginary part.
   a. Thing
   b. Complex number0
   c. Undefined
   d. Undefined

24. The _____ of a positive integer are the prime numbers that divide into that integer exactly, without leaving a remainder. The process of finding these numbers is called integer factorization, or prime factorization.
   a. Prime factor0
   b. Thing
   c. Undefined
   d. Undefined

25. In mathematics, a _____ is the result of multiplying, or an expression that identifies factors to be multiplied.
   a. Product0
   b. Thing
   c. Undefined
   d. Undefined

26. In mathematics, factorization (British English: factorisation) or factoring is the decomposition of an object (for example, a number, a polynomial, or a matrix) into a product of other objects, or _____, which when multiplied together give the original.
   a. Thing
   b. Factors0
   c. Undefined
   d. Undefined

27. _____ has many meanings, most of which simply .
   a. Thing
   b. Power0
   c. Undefined
   d. Undefined

28. In a mathematical proof or a syllogism, a _____ is a statement that is the logical consequence of preceding statements.

Chapter 9. FACTORIZATION

a. Conclusion0
b. Concept
c. Undefined
d. Undefined

29. The _____, the average in everyday English, which is also called the arithmetic _____ (and is distinguished from the geometric _____ or harmonic _____). The average is also called the sample _____. The expected value of a random variable, which is also called the population _____.
a. Thing
b. Mean0
c. Undefined
d. Undefined

30. In mathematics, an _____ .
a. Thing
b. Ellipse0
c. Undefined
d. Undefined

31. In mathematics, the concept of a _____ tries to capture the intuitive idea of a geometrical one-dimensional and continuous object. A simple example is the circle.
a. Curve0
b. Thing
c. Undefined
d. Undefined

32. In mathematics, _____ are the intuitive idea of a geometrical one-dimensional and continuous object.
a. Curves0
b. Thing
c. Undefined
d. Undefined

33. In abstract algebra, something that is _____ over a ring is a generalization of the notion of vector space, where instead of requiring the scalars to lie in a field, the "scalars" may lie in an arbitrary ring.
a. Modular0
b. Concept
c. Undefined
d. Undefined

34. There are two main approaches to _____ in mathematics. They are the model theory of _____ and the proof theory of _____.
a. Thing
b. Truth0
c. Undefined
d. Undefined

35. _____ (Groups, Algorithms and Programming) is a computer algebra system for computational discrete algebra with particular emphasis on, but not restricted to, computational group theory.
a. Thing
b. Gap0
c. Undefined
d. Undefined

36. A _____ of a number is the product of that number with any integer.
a. Multiple0
b. Thing
c. Undefined
d. Undefined

37. In set theory and other branches of mathematics, the _____ of a collection of sets is the set that contains everything that belongs to any of the sets, but nothing else.
a. Union0
b. Thing
c. Undefined
d. Undefined

Chapter 9. FACTORIZATION

38. The _____ are finiteness properties statisfied by certain algebraic structures, most importantly, ideals in a commutatice rings inthe works of David Hilbert, Emmy Nöther, and Emil Artin.
    a. Thing
    b. Ascending chain condition0
    c. Undefined
    d. Undefined

39. A _____ fraction is a fraction in which the absolute value of the numerator is less than the denominator--hence, the absolute value of the fraction is less than 1.
    a. Thing
    b. Proper0
    c. Undefined
    d. Undefined

40. In mathematics, a set is called _____ if there is a bijection between the set and some set of the form {1, 2, ..., n} where n is a natural number.
    a. Thing
    b. Finite0
    c. Undefined
    d. Undefined

41. Compass and straightedge or ruler-and-compass _____ is the _____ of lengths or angles using only an idealized ruler and compass.
    a. Construction0
    b. Thing
    c. Undefined
    d. Undefined

42. In mathematics, science including computer science, linguistics and engineering, an _____ is, generally speaking, an independent variable or input to a function.
    a. Thing
    b. Argument0
    c. Undefined
    d. Undefined

43. A _____ is a mathematical statement which follows easily from a previously proven statement, typically a mathematical theorem.
    a. Thing
    b. Corollary0
    c. Undefined
    d. Undefined

44. _____ or arithmetics is the oldest and most elementary branch of mathematics, used by almost everyone, for tasks ranging from simple daily counting to advanced science and business calculations.
    a. Thing
    b. Arithmetic0
    c. Undefined
    d. Undefined

45. In number theory, the _____ of arithmetic (or unique factorization theorem) states that every natural number greater than 1 can be written as a unique product of prime numbers.
    a. Concept
    b. Fundamental theorem0
    c. Undefined
    d. Undefined

46. In number theory, the _____ states that every natural number greater than 1 can be written as a unique product of prime numbers.
    a. Concept
    b. Fundamental Theorem of Arithmetic0
    c. Undefined
    d. Undefined

Chapter 9. FACTORIZATION

47. In mathematics, computing, linguistics, and related disciplines, an _____ is a finite list of well-defined instructions for accomplishing some task which, given an initial state, will terminate in a defined end-state.
   a. Algorithm0
   b. Concept
   c. Undefined
   d. Undefined

48. The _____ is a theorem in mathematics which precisely expresses the outcome of the usual process of division of integers. The name is something of a misnomer, as it is a theorem, not an algorithm, i.e. a well-defined procedure for achieving a specific task — although the _____ can be used to find the greatest common divisor of two integers.
   a. Division Algorithm0
   b. Thing
   c. Undefined
   d. Undefined

49. In mathematics, a _____ is the end result of a division problem. It can also be expressed as the number of times the divisor divides into the dividend.
   a. Thing
   b. Quotient0
   c. Undefined
   d. Undefined

50. In mathematics, the _____ divisor of two non-zero integers, is the largest positive integer that divides both numbers without remainder.
   a. Greatest common0
   b. Thing
   c. Undefined
   d. Undefined

51. In mathematics, a _____ of an integer n, also called a factor of n, is an integer which evenly divides n without leaving a remainder.
   a. Thing
   b. Divisor0
   c. Undefined
   d. Undefined

52. In mathematics, the notion of _____ is a generalization of the notion of invertible.
   a. Thing
   b. Cancellation0
   c. Undefined
   d. Undefined

53. In mathematics, a _____ is an expression that is constructed from one or more variables and constants, using only the operations of addition, subtraction, multiplication, and constant positive whole number exponents. is a _____. Note in particular that division by an expression containing a variable is not in general allowed in polynomials. [1]
   a. Polynomial0
   b. Thing
   c. Undefined
   d. Undefined

54. In mathematics, a _____ is a constant multiplicative factor of a certain object. The object can be such things as a variable, a vector, a function, etc. For example, the _____ of $9x^2$ is 9.
   a. Thing
   b. Coefficient0
   c. Undefined
   d. Undefined

55. In mathematics, there are several meanings of _____ depending on the subject.
   a. Thing
   b. Degree0
   c. Undefined
   d. Undefined

Chapter 9. FACTORIZATION

56. _____ Logic is a concept in traditional logic referring to a "type of immediate inference in which from a given proposition another proposition is inferred which has as its subject the predicate of the original proposition and as its predicate the subject of the original proposition (the quality of the proposition being retained)."
   a. Concept
   b. Converse0
   c. Undefined
   d. Undefined

57. In mathematics, an inequality is a statement about the relative size or order of two objects. For example 14 > 10, or 14 is _____ 10.
   a. Thing
   b. Greater than0
   c. Undefined
   d. Undefined

58. In mathematics and the mathematical sciences, a _____ is a fixed, but possibly unspecified, value. This is in contrast to a variable, which is not fixed.
   a. Thing
   b. Constant0
   c. Undefined
   d. Undefined

59. In mathematics, _____ is an elementary arithmetic operation. When one of the numbers is a whole number, _____ is the repeated sum of the other number.
   a. Multiplication0
   b. Thing
   c. Undefined
   d. Undefined

60. In mathematics, a _____ is an ordered list of objects. Like a set, it contains members, also called elements or terms, and the number of terms is called the length of the _____. Unlike a set, order matters, and the exact same elements can appear multiple times at different positions in the _____.
   a. Thing
   b. Sequence0
   c. Undefined
   d. Undefined

61. Equivalence is the condition of being _____ or essentially equal.
   a. Thing
   b. Equivalent0
   c. Undefined
   d. Undefined

62. In mathematics, a _____ occurs if there is a bijection between the set and some set of the form 1, 2, ..., n where n is a natural number.
   a. Finite set0
   b. Concept
   c. Undefined
   d. Undefined

63. In mathematics, the _____ of two sets A and B is the set that contains all elements of A that also belong to B (or equivalently, all elements of B that also belong to A), but no other elements.
   a. Thing
   b. Intersection0
   c. Undefined
   d. Undefined

64. The mathematical concept of a _____ expresses the intuitive idea of deterministic dependence between two quantities, one of which is viewed as primary and the other as secondary. A _____ then is a way to associate a unique output for each input of a specified type, for example, a real number or an element of a given set.

Chapter 9. FACTORIZATION

a. Thing
b. Function0
c. Undefined
d. Undefined

65. A _____ is the result of the addition of a set of numbers. The numbers may be natural numbers, complex numbers, matrices, or still more complicated objects. An infinite _____ is a subtle procedure known as a series.
a. Thing
b. Sum0
c. Undefined
d. Undefined

66. _____ is electromagnetic radiation with a wavelength that is visible to the eye (visible _____) or, in a technical or scientific context, electromagnetic radiation of any wavelength.
a. Thing
b. Light0
c. Undefined
d. Undefined

67. _____, also known as _____ of Alexandria, was a Greek mathematician. His Elements is the most successful textbook in the history of mathematics. In it, the principles of geometry are deduced from a small set of axioms. His method of proving mathematical theorems by logical reasoning from accepted first principles remains the backbone of mathematics and is responsible for the field's characteristic rigor
a. Person
b. Euclid0
c. Undefined
d. Undefined

68. In number theory, the _____ is an algorithm to determine the greatest common divisor. Its major significance is that it does not require factoring the two integers, and it is also significant in that it is one of the oldest algorithms known, dating back to the ancient Greeks.
a. Thing
b. Euclidean algorithm0
c. Undefined
d. Undefined

69. The _____ of a mathematical object is its size: a property by which it can be larger or smaller than other objects of the same kind; in technical terms, an ordering of the class of objects to which it belongs.
a. Thing
b. Magnitude0
c. Undefined
d. Undefined

70. A _____ is a function that assigns a number to subsets of a given set.
a. Thing
b. Measure0
c. Undefined
d. Undefined

71. _____ was an Indian mathematician and astronomer.
a. Person
b. Brahmagupta0
c. Undefined
d. Undefined

72. A _____ is the part of the dividend that is left over when the dividend is not evenly divisible by the divisor.
a. Thing
b. Remainder0
c. Undefined
d. Undefined

73. As an abstract term, _____ means similarity between objects.

Chapter 9. FACTORIZATION

    a. Congruence0
    b. Thing
    c. Undefined
    d. Undefined

74. In geometry, two sets are called _____ if one can be transformed into the other by an isometry, i.e., a combination of translations, rotations and reflections.
    a. Thing
    b. Congruent0
    c. Undefined
    d. Undefined

75. The _____ integers are all the integers from zero on upwards.
    a. Thing
    b. Nonnegative0
    c. Undefined
    d. Undefined

76. _____ is the fee paid on borrowed money.
    a. Thing
    b. Interest0
    c. Undefined
    d. Undefined

77. In mathematics, the _____ (or modulus) of a real number is its numerical value without regard to its sign.
    a. Thing
    b. Absolute value0
    c. Undefined
    d. Undefined

78. The _____ of two integers is the smallest positive integer that is a multiple of both intergers.
    a. Least common multiple0
    b. Thing
    c. Undefined
    d. Undefined

79. In common philosophical language, a proposition or _____, is the content of an assertion, that is, it is true-or-false and defined by the meaning of a particular piece of language.
    a. Concept
    b. Statement0
    c. Undefined
    d. Undefined

80. The easiest _____ prime numbers resides in the use of the Sieve of Eratosthenes, an algorithm that discovers all prime numbers to a specified integer.
    a. Method for finding0
    b. Thing
    c. Undefined
    d. Undefined

81. _____ is bother the congnitive process of transferring information from a particular subject , and a linguistic expression corresponding to such a process.
    a. Analogy0
    b. Thing
    c. Undefined
    d. Undefined

82. In mathematics, a _____ number is a number which can be expressed as a ratio of two integers. Non-integer _____ numbers (commonly called fractions) are usually written as the vulgar fraction a / b, where b is not zero.
    a. Rational0
    b. Thing
    c. Undefined
    d. Undefined

83. A _____ is a set whose members are members of another set or a set contained within another set.

Chapter 9. FACTORIZATION

a. Subset0
b. Thing
c. Undefined
d. Undefined

84. _____ is a natural number that has exactly two distinct natural number divisors, which are 1 and the _____ itself.
   a. Thing
   b. Prime number0
   c. Undefined
   d. Undefined

85. _____ traditionally refers to the statistical process of determining comparable scores on different forms of an exam
   a. Thing
   b. Equating0
   c. Undefined
   d. Undefined

86. In plane geometry, a _____ is a polygon with four equal sides, four right angles, and parallel opposite sides. In algebra, the _____ of a number is that number multiplied by itself.
   a. Square0
   b. Thing
   c. Undefined
   d. Undefined

Chapter 10. AUTOMORPHISMS AND GALOIS THEORY

1. The most important measure of central tendency, and one of the basic building blocks of all statistical analysis, is the arithmetic _____. It is simply the sum of all the set of values divided by the number of values involved. As a measure of central tendency, it is affected by extreme scores, and it assumes a ratio scale of measurement.
   a. -equivalence
   b. Mean1
   c. Undefined
   d. Undefined

2. Horizontal axis of display containing the trailing digits is called _____.
   a. Leaves1
   b. -equivalence
   c. Undefined
   d. Undefined

3. The probability of correctly rejecting a false Ho is referred to as _____.
   a. Power1
   b. -equivalence
   c. Undefined
   d. Undefined

4. Another word for independent variables in the analysis of variance is _____.
   a. -equivalence
   b. Factors1
   c. Undefined
   d. Undefined

5. _____ is used synonymously for variable.
   a. -equivalence
   b. Factor1
   c. Undefined
   d. Undefined

6. A number that does not change in value in a given situation is a _____.
   a. Constant1
   b. -equivalence
   c. Undefined
   d. Undefined

7. _____ is implied when data values are distributed in the same way above and below the middle of the sample.
   a. -equivalence
   b. Symmetry1
   c. Undefined
   d. Undefined

8. The goal of most inferential statistical analyses is to be able to generalize or apply the findings to the entire population and not just to the sample. The concept of _____ requires that the researcher determine some level of probability that the findings were due to chance or that they actually describe the population. The value of the probability that the findings were due to chance is usually reported when the findings of an analysis is reported.
   a. -equivalence
   b. Generalization1
   c. Undefined
   d. Undefined

ANSWER KEY

Chapter 1

1. a	2. a	3. a	4. b	5. b	6. a	7. b	8. b	9. b	10. a
11. b	12. a	13. a	14. b	15. b	16. b	17. a	18. b	19. a	20. a
21. b	22. a	23. a	24. a	25. b	26. a	27. b	28. a	29. b	30. a
31. a	32. a	33. a	34. b	35. a	36. a	37. a	38. b	39. b	40. a
41. b	42. a	43. a	44. b	45. a	46. a	47. a	48. a	49. b	50. b
51. b	52. b	53. a	54. a	55. a	56. a	57. b	58. b	59. a	60. b
61. a	62. a	63. b	64. b	65. b	66. a	67. a	68. b	69. a	70. b
71. b	72. a	73. b	74. a	75. b	76. a	77. a	78. a	79. a	80. b
81. a	82. a	83. b	84. b	85. b	86. a	87. a	88. b	89. a	90. a
91. a	92. a	93. b	94. a	95. a	96. a	97. a	98. a	99. b	100. a
101. b	102. a	103. b	104. a	105. a	106. a	107. b	108. b	109. a	110. a
111. a	112. b	113. a	114. b	115. b	116. b	117. b	118. a	119. b	120. a
121. a	122. b	123. a	124. b	125. a	126. b	127. b	128. a	129. b	130. a
131. b	132. a	133. b	134. a	135. a	136. b	137. b	138. a	139. b	140. b
141. b	142. a	143. b	144. a	145. b	146. b	147. a	148. b	149. b	150. a
151. a	152. a	153. b	154. b	155. b	156. a	157. a	158. a	159. a	160. a
161. b	162. a	163. b	164. a	165. a	166. a	167. a			

Chapter 2

1. b	2. b	3. b	4. a	5. a	6. a	7. b	8. b	9. a	10. a
11. b	12. a	13. a	14. a	15. b	16. b	17. a	18. a	19. b	20. a
21. a	22. a	23. b	24. b	25. a	26. b	27. b	28. b	29. b	30. a
31. a	32. b	33. b	34. b	35. b	36. a	37. b	38. b	39. b	40. a
41. a	42. a	43. b	44. b	45. a	46. a	47. a	48. b	49. b	50. a
51. a	52. b	53. a	54. a	55. a	56. b	57. b	58. b	59. b	60. b
61. b	62. b	63. b	64. a	65. b	66. b	67. b	68. b	69. b	70. b
71. b	72. a	73. a	74. b	75. a	76. b	77. b	78. a	79. a	80. a
81. b	82. b	83. b	84. b	85. b	86. b	87. b	88. a	89. a	90. a
91. a	92. a	93. b	94. a	95. a	96. b	97. a	98. a	99. a	100. b
101. b	102. b	103. b	104. b	105. b	106. b	107. a	108. a	109. a	110. a
111. a	112. a	113. b	114. b	115. a	116. a	117. b	118. a	119. a	120. b
121. a	122. a	123. b	124. b	125. a	126. b	127. a	128. a	129. a	130. b
131. a	132. a	133. b	134. a	135. a	136. a	137. b	138. b	139. a	

Chapter 3

1. a	2. a	3. a	4. a	5. a	6. a	7. a	8. b	9. b	10. b
11. a	12. b	13. b	14. a	15. a	16. a	17. a	18. a	19. a	20. b
21. a	22. a	23. a	24. b	25. b	26. b	27. a	28. b	29. b	30. b
31. b	32. a	33. b	34. b	35. a	36. b	37. b	38. b	39. a	40. a
41. a	42. a	43. b	44. b	45. b	46. b	47. a	48. a	49. a	50. b
51. a	52. a	53. b	54. a	55. a	56. b	57. a	58. b	59. b	60. b
61. b	62. b	63. a	64. a	65. b	66. a	67. b	68. b	69. b	70. b
71. b	72. b	73. b	74. a	75. b	76. b	77. b	78. b	79. b	80. a
81. b	82. a	83. b	84. a	85. b	86. b	87. b	88. b	89. a	90. b
91. a	92. b	93. b	94. a	95. a	96. a	97. b	98. b	99. b	100. b
101. b	102. b	103. b	104. b	105. a	106. b	107. b	108. a	109. b	110. b
111. a	112. a	113. a	114. b	115. b	116. a	117. b	118. b	119. a	120. b
121. b	122. a	123. a	124. b	125. a	126. b	127. b	128. b	129. b	130. b
131. a	132. b	133. a	134. a	135. a	136. b	137. b			

Chapter 4

1. a	2. b	3. b	4. b	5. a	6. a	7. a	8. a	9. a	10. a
11. a	12. b	13. a	14. a	15. b	16. a	17. a	18. b	19. a	20. a
21. b	22. a	23. a	24. a	25. b	26. a	27. b	28. a	29. b	30. a
31. a	32. a	33. b	34. a	35. a	36. a	37. a	38. a	39. b	40. b
41. b	42. a	43. b	44. a	45. b	46. b	47. a	48. a	49. a	50. a
51. b	52. b	53. b	54. a	55. a	56. a	57. b	58. b	59. a	60. b
61. a	62. b	63. b	64. b	65. a	66. a	67. a	68. b	69. a	70. a
71. b	72. a	73. b	74. a	75. a	76. a	77. a	78. b	79. a	80. a
81. b	82. b	83. b	84. a	85. a	86. b	87. b	88. b	89. a	90. b
91. a	92. b	93. b	94. a	95. b	96. a	97. a	98. b	99. b	100. a
101. b	102. a	103. b	104. a	105. a	106. a	107. a	108. a	109. b	110. a
111. b	112. a	113. b	114. a	115. b	116. a	117. b	118. b	119. b	120. b
121. a	122. a	123. b	124. b	125. a	126. a	127. a	128. b	129. b	130. b
131. a	132. a	133. b	134. a	135. a	136. b	137. a	138. b	139. b	140. a
141. b	142. a	143. a	144. a	145. a	146. a	147. a	148. a	149. a	150. a
151. a	152. b	153. a	154. b	155. b	156. b	157. a	158. b	159. b	160. b
161. b	162. b	163. b							

Chapter 5

1. b	2. a	3. a	4. a	5. a	6. b	7. b	8. b	9. a	10. b
11. b	12. b	13. b	14. a	15. b	16. a	17. b	18. b	19. b	20. a
21. b	22. b	23. a	24. a	25. b	26. b	27. b	28. a	29. b	30. a
31. a	32. a	33. a	34. a	35. b	36. b	37. b	38. a	39. a	40. a
41. a	42. a	43. a	44. b	45. b	46. b	47. b	48. b	49. a	50. b
51. b	52. a	53. b	54. b	55. b	56. a	57. a	58. a	59. b	60. a
61. a	62. b	63. a	64. b	65. b	66. b	67. a	68. b	69. b	70. a
71. b	72. b	73. a	74. b	75. a	76. b	77. a	78. a	79. a	80. b
81. a	82. a	83. a	84. b						

ANSWER KEY

Chapter 6

1. b	2. a	3. a	4. a	5. a	6. b	7. a	8. b	9. a	10. b
11. b	12. a	13. a	14. a	15. a	16. a	17. b	18. a	19. b	20. a
21. b	22. a	23. a	24. a	25. a	26. a	27. a	28. b	29. b	30. a
31. a	32. a	33. a	34. a	35. b	36. a	37. a	38. a	39. a	40. a
41. b	42. b	43. a	44. a	45. b	46. b	47. b	48. b	49. b	50. a
51. b	52. b	53. a	54. a	55. b	56. a	57. a	58. b	59. b	60. b
61. a	62. a	63. a	64. a	65. a	66. a	67. b	68. a	69. a	70. b
71. b	72. b	73. a	74. a	75. a	76. a	77. a	78. a	79. a	80. a
81. b	82. b	83. b	84. a	85. a	86. b	87. b	88. b	89. a	90. a
91. a	92. b	93. b	94. a	95. b	96. b	97. a	98. a	99. a	100. a
101. b	102. b	103. a	104. a	105. a	106. b	107. a	108. b	109. a	110. b
111. b	112. a	113. b	114. b	115. b	116. a	117. a	118. a	119. b	120. b

Chapter 7

1. a	2. b	3. b	4. a	5. b	6. b	7. b	8. b	9. b	10. a
11. a	12. a	13. a	14. b	15. b	16. a	17. b	18. b	19. a	20. b
21. a	22. b	23. a	24. a	25. a	26. a	27. b	28. a	29. b	30. a
31. b	32. b	33. b	34. b	35. b	36. a	37. b	38. a	39. a	40. a
41. a	42. a	43. a	44. b	45. b	46. a	47. b	48. b	49. b	50. b
51. a	52. b	53. b	54. b	55. a	56. a	57. a	58. a	59. b	60. a
61. a	62. a	63. b	64. a	65. a	66. b	67. b	68. b	69. b	70. a
71. b	72. b	73. b	74. a	75. b	76. a	77. b	78. a	79. a	80. b
81. b	82. b	83. b	84. a	85. a	86. a	87. a	88. b	89. b	90. a
91. b	92. a	93. b	94. a	95. b	96. b	97. a	98. a	99. a	100. b

Chapter 8

1. a	2. b	3. b	4. b	5. b	6. b	7. a	8. a	9. a	10. b
11. a	12. b	13. b	14. a	15. a	16. b	17. a	18. b	19. a	20. a
21. b	22. b	23. b	24. b	25. b	26. b	27. b	28. a	29. b	30. b
31. b	32. a	33. a	34. b	35. b	36. b	37. a	38. b	39. a	40. a
41. b	42. a	43. b	44. b	45. b	46. a	47. a	48. b	49. b	50. a
51. a	52. a	53. b	54. b	55. a	56. b	57. b	58. a	59. b	60. b
61. a	62. a	63. a	64. b	65. b	66. b	67. b	68. b	69. b	70. a
71. a	72. b	73. b	74. b	75. b	76. a	77. a	78. b	79. a	80. a
81. b	82. b	83. b	84. a	85. a	86. b	87. b	88. a	89. b	90. b
91. b	92. a	93. a	94. b						

Chapter 9

1. a	2. b	3. b	4. b	5. a	6. a	7. a	8. a	9. b	10. b
11. b	12. b	13. a	14. b	15. a	16. b	17. a	18. a	19. a	20. a
21. a	22. a	23. b	24. a	25. a	26. b	27. b	28. a	29. b	30. b
31. a	32. a	33. a	34. b	35. b	36. a	37. a	38. b	39. b	40. b
41. a	42. b	43. b	44. b	45. b	46. b	47. a	48. a	49. b	50. a
51. b	52. b	53. a	54. b	55. b	56. b	57. b	58. b	59. a	60. b
61. b	62. a	63. b	64. b	65. b	66. b	67. b	68. b	69. b	70. b
71. b	72. b	73. a	74. b	75. b	76. b	77. b	78. a	79. b	80. a
81. a	82. a	83. a	84. b	85. b	86. a				

Chapter 10

1. b	2. a	3. a	4. b	5. b	6. a	7. b	8. b

www.ingramcontent.com/pod-product-compliance
Lightning Source LLC
Chambersburg PA
CBHW082046230426
43670CB00016B/2800